Introduction

This book is designed to help you easily teach New Testament scriptures to your kids in fun and meaningful ways! Here's how it works:

- There are 52 activities to aid you in making scripture learning experiences fun, engaging, and meaningful for kids (one for each week of the year).

- Each activity has two parts: the lesson instructions at the beginning of the book and the corresponding Activity Sheets at the end of the book.

- The lesson instruction pages at the beginning of the book elaborate on ways you can make each activity engaging and meaningful. The Activity Sheets are designed so that you can cut them straight out of the book and put them to immediate use.

- The activities follow the order of scripture study as laid out by the Come, Follow Me curriculum and are designed to benefit anyone who is studying the New Testament.

Activity Sheet:

Lesson Instruction Page:

WEEK 1
MATTHEW 1; LUKE 1

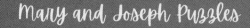

Mary and Joseph Puzzles

The New Testament teaches us about some amazing people! We're going to put together two puzzles to see if we can guess who two of these amazing people are. Start with the Mary puzzle, and then do the Joseph puzzle.

Cut out the Mary puzzle pieces from the Week 1 Activity Sheet. Without looking, each person will pull out one piece at a time. As they pull each piece out, read the scripture hint for that number, talk about what it means, and apply it to ourselves. Then follow the same process for the Joseph puzzle. Ask questions like:

> She was afraid of the angel. Are you ever afraid of things too?

> The angel told her that the Lord was with her. Do you think the Lord is with us in our lives too?

> She said she would do what the Lord wanted her to do. What are some things the Lord wants you to do? Are they difficult to do sometimes?

When the puzzles are complete, discuss why the Savior needed to be born to a mortal mother, and explain that His Father (Heavenly Father) is immortal. Share testimonies of Him and the importance of His mission on Earth.

52 WEEKS of NEW TESTAMENT ACTIVITIES

Ready-to-Use Activity Sheets for
Simple, Fun & Meaningful Child Lessons

MITZI SCHONEMAN

CFI • An imprint of Cedar Fort, Inc. • Springville, Utah

Thank You!

A billion thanks to the friends and family who helped make this book a reality.

We love you.

ISBN 13: 978-1-4621-4484-6

Published by CFI, an imprint of Cedar Fort, Inc.
2373 W. 700 S., Suite 100, Springville, UT 84663
Distributed by Cedar Fort, Inc., www.cedarfort.com

Cover design by Shawnda T. Craig
Cover design © 2022 Cedar Fort, Inc.

Printed in Colombia

10 9 8 7 6 5 4 3 2 1

Printed on acid-free paper

Look at photos of each kid from when they were younger. Share fun memories and stories. Do you think Jesus was ever a kid? What do you think He was like? There is one scripture story about Him when He was young. Read/summarize/discuss Luke 2:40–52. What did He mean when He said He was doing His Father's business? Who is His Father?

Share pictures and stories of the places where each kid was born. How do you think your births were the same/different from the birth of Jesus Christ? Since He is such an important person, do you think He was born in a pretty important place? Read Luke 2:1–7 and tell them to listen carefully to where Jesus was laid after He was born. Discuss the humble circumstances of His birth. Testify of how He came to Earth to help every one of us, regardless of our circumstances.

Teddy Bear Theater

Use props with teddy bears/dolls to act out the story of the birth of Jesus. Read Luke 2:8–38 (summarize parts as needed) and Matthew 2:1–12. Have the kids listen as you read so they can act out the different parts with their teddy bears. Use the props on the Week 2 Activity Sheet, and let them find additional household items to dress their teddy bears up more, such as dishcloths for head coverings.

Hidden Picture Game (People We Know)

Give everyone a blank frame from the Week 3 Activity Sheet. Have them draw a picture inside their frame of someone they know well (a family member/Church leader/Cookie Monster/a favorite T.V. character/etc.). Choose one person at a time to go out of the room while another person hides their own picture somewhere in the room. When the person comes back, give them hints about the person they're searching for before they start looking to see if they can guess who it is they're supposed to find (what they look like, what they like to eat, etc.). Then let them start searching, and tell them if they're hot or cold to help them find it.

If time permits, you could print up real photographs of people for them to search for.

Hidden Picture Game (Jesus)

After each person has had a turn, hide the picture of Jesus from the Week 3 Activity Sheet somewhere in the room and follow the same process. Possible hints could be: It's someone who healed many people when He was on the earth. It's someone who has made many miracles happen. It's someone who loves you very much. It's someone who made it possible for us to live together as a family forever.

DISCUSS

Explain that when Jesus came to Earth over 2,000 years ago, not everyone knew who He was or where He was at first. Lots of people had been waiting for Him to come to Earth. How do you think they knew it was really Him when He came? Did other people say "hot/cold" to let them know if they'd found Jesus? Summarize how some people chose to "come and see" Jesus in the end of John 1. Verses that could be focused on include:

John 1:29–34	John 1:35–42	John 1:43–51

Jesus invites us to also "come and see" for ourselves (John 1:39). Can we see where Jesus lives right now? How can we "come and see" Him now? How do we feel when we're close to Him? Do people tell us we're "hot/cold"? How can we help others "come and see" Jesus and know that He is our Savior? Share ways we can learn more about Him while we're alive and testify that He is there for us in our lives, even when we don't see Him.

Review what we know about Mary. What was her cousin's name (Elisabeth)? Elisabeth and her husband, Zacharias, prayed for a child. After waiting for a long time, they were blessed with one. They named their baby John, and he later became known as John the Baptist. His mission was to prepare the minds and hearts of the people to receive the Savior. His main message was for people to repent (Matthew 3:2). True repentance means we turn our hearts and will to Heavenly Father and Jesus Christ.

1. Fold the picture of Jesus on the Week 4 Activity Sheet so that it stands up. Place it in the middle of a table.

2. Cut the cards out from the "Turning Our Hearts and Minds toward Jesus Christ" Week 4 Activity Sheet and place them upside down in a pile.

3. Set out some playdough.

4. Let each person take turns choosing a card from the pile.

5. After answering their question, give them a small piece of the playdough. If their card has a picture of a heart, they will mold their lump into a heart. If it has a picture of a brain, they'll mold it into a brain. Place the playdough hearts and minds around the picture of Jesus.

6. Discuss how blessed we are when we turn our hearts and minds to Jesus.

   To simplify, skip the playdough step and have each person place their cards around Jesus after answering each question.

What changes might we need to make in order to keep our lives more pointed toward Jesus Christ? Encourage everyone to pray about one thing they can alter in their lives in order to have Christ in their hearts and minds and become more like Him.

WEEK 5
MATTHEW 4; LUKE 4–5

Jesus Christ's Mission

Jesus Christ had a very important mission to fulfill during His time on Earth. Satan tried to make Him doubt who He was by stating, *"If* thou be the Son of God" (Luke 4:3) and tempted Christ to worship him instead of God. Read Luke 4:1–13 and summarize how Jesus responded to Satan.

Jesus Christ was blessed with "power of the Spirit" (Luke 4:14) after this experience. List things He did through the power of the Spirit as stated in Luke 4:18 and Matthew 4:23–24.

OUR MISSION: We also have very important things we need to do during our time on Earth. Jesus Christ can help us do those things when we trust Him and follow Him. How can we stand strong against Satan's attempts to cause us to doubt who we are and who Christ is?

FISHING STORY: Read Luke 5:1–11, then act out the story. In what ways were Jesus's disciples blessed by doing what He asked them to do? Luke 5:11 states that they "forsook all" to follow Christ. What things might we need to forsake in our lives in order to follow Christ?

Boat Activity

Cut out the boats on the Week 5 Activity Sheet. Each person will choose one specific way they will follow Christ this week and draw it on the side of their boat. Discuss blessings that we receive from Christ when we follow Him. Fill each boat up with crackers or candies shaped like fish to represent these blessings.

TESTIFY

Testify of Jesus Christ's love for each one of us and of His desire to bless and help us.

Instead of crackers and candy, you can also have each person cut out fish-shaped pieces of paper. On each fish, write specific blessings we've seen in our lives from following Christ.

Give everyone a drink of water. How does water make our bodies stronger? Why is it good for us? Explain that this week's lesson talks lots about water!

Just like water is important to us and keeps us alive, Heavenly Father knew that we needed Christ in our lives. He keeps our spirits strong, and He saves us from physical and spiritual death. Read and discuss John 3:16–17.

Musical Envelope Activity

Cut out the "Musical Envelope" pieces from the Week 6 Activity Sheet and place them in 3 separate envelopes. On the outside of each envelope, write #1, #2, and #3. Depending on the attention span of your kids, you could also put a small treat into each envelope to help keep their attention. Have everyone sit in a circle and hand out the envelopes randomly. Play a song, such as "He Sent His Son," while people pass the envelopes around the circle. Stop the music at random times. The first time you stop, whoever is holding #1 will open it. Read what's on the sheet and do the listed activity. Follow the same process again for envelopes #2 and #3.

TESTIFY

After the musical envelopes activity, testify of how Christ and His gospel are just as important to us as water. Christ is needed in our lives, and He can change us to become as He is.

Jesus Christ taught us how to find lasting happiness. Explain that "blessed" means "happy." Have everyone practice showing the biggest smiles they can.

Read Matthew 5:1–12 and Luke 6:20–26. Ask them to smile each time they hear the word "blessed." Talk about each attribute mentioned in these verses in as much depth as desired. How are we happier when we live our lives in these ways?

If the kids you are teaching are old enough, you could give them a quiz to see if they remember which specific attributes bring certain blessings (Who did Christ say will obtain mercy? Who will see God? Etc.).

Peacemakers

Cut out the scenarios on the Week 7 Activity Sheet. Each person will take turns choosing one out of an upside-down pile and role-playing how they could respond in a peace-making way. If the response is done in a way that would help make peace, that person can color in one letter on the large "Peace Maker" sign. Talk about how when we all work together to be peacemakers, we can all be happier and blessed.

Testify of the importance of being peacemakers and becoming more like Christ. Challenge each person to find ways to be peacemakers in every situation in the coming weeks.

Another option: Instead of having each person color on the "Peacemaker" heart after role-playing peace-making scenarios, have them use any hands-on items you can find to build the word "Peace" with (blocks, popsicle sticks, play dough, candy hearts, etc.).

EXTENSION

Read and discuss ways we can be peacemakers as found in Luke 6:27–31.

The Savior urges us to not only listen to His teachings, but to also live our lives by them. When our lives and actions are built upon the principles He has taught, they give us a strong foundation that can help us withstand the winds and floods that will come into our lives.

Sing "The Wise Man and the Foolish Man." Touch a solid rock and compare it to sand.

Cut apart the strips on the Week 8 Activity Sheet and assemble the houses from the second Week 8 Activity Sheet. Take turns choosing one strip out of a bag or an upside-down pile. If it's something that shows that your foundation is built upon Christ, put it inside the house with the picture of Christ. If not, put it inside the other house. Place the house with the picture of Christ on a large, solid rock. Place the other house on sand while discussing Matthew 7:24–27.

DISCUSS

What kinds of winds and floods might come to us in our lives? Testify of how Christ and His teachings can help us when the difficult times come.

EXTENSION

On a large rock, write or paint a picture of a specific way you plan to build your spiritual foundation on the rock of Christ's gospel or one of His teachings that is especially meaningful to you.

WEEK 9
MATTHEW 8; MARK 4

Water Bottle Storms

Play storm sounds in the background while everyone closes their eyes. Tell them to think about a time when they were scared or worried about something. How did that experience feel like a storm? Who can help us feel comfort during those times? Share stories if desired.

Story Sequence and Pictures

Cut out the sequence cards from the Week 9 Activity Sheet. Fold each one so they stand up like tents. Put them in order and read them one at a time. As each card is read, take turns drawing pictures on the back to represent that part of the story. Discuss how they would have felt if they were there. Then let everyone take turns summarizing the story by looking at the pictures. You could also read Matthew 8:23–27 while looking at the pictures to see how this account of the story compares to the one in Mark 4.

Water Bottle Activity

Give each person a water bottle with no label on it. Take turns shaking the bottle while sharing something we might go through in our lives that is difficult or scary. Share ways Jesus might either calm the storm for us or help us feel peace in our hearts. Then have everyone shake their water bottles while walking in a circle and listening to/singing "Master, the Tempest is Raging." Designate one person to be "The Calmer." That person will hold up a picture of Jesus Christ at random times throughout the song. Everyone else will race to see who can freeze the quickest. Let others have turns being "The Calmer."

After everyone has had a turn, give each person a "Jesus Christ Can Calm the Troubled Waters of Our Lives" label from the Week 9 Activity Sheet to tape onto their water bottle (quote from President Howard W. Hunter). Testify of Christ's ability to help calm storms around us and to help calm our hearts inside of us when those storms outside of us haven't stopped yet. Discuss things we can do to feel His peace in our lives and testify of His love for us and His desire to help us.

EXTENSION

Let everyone use a dry erase marker to write/draw specific things on their water bottle that scare or worry them. Explain that those scary and worrisome things might not always be taken away when we'd like them to, but Jesus Christ can help us feel calm and peaceful on the inside through those times.

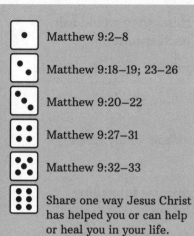

Matthew 9:2–8

Matthew 9:18–19; 23–26

Matthew 9:20–22

Matthew 9:27–31

Matthew 9:32–33

Share one way Jesus Christ has helped you or can help or heal you in your life.

As word of Christ's power spread, many people came to Him asking for His healing power to bless them.

Take turns rolling a die. Based on the number that is rolled, read the corresponding scripture verses and summarize who Christ healed in those verses and how they were healed. If a number that has already been read is rolled again, that person will summarize the corresponding story without reading the scripture verses again.

Apostles

Because so many people needed spiritual and physical help, Jesus Christ called Twelve Apostles and "gave them power" (Matthew 10:1). He instructed them to preach as well as to heal others (Matthew 10:7–8). Cut out the picture of Jesus and the Twelve Apostles from the Week 10 Activity Sheet. Read Matthew 10:2–4. As you read, have the kids listen for the names of each of Christ's original Twelve Apostles. As they hear each name, they can place that Apostle next to the picture of Jesus.

Explain that the word *apostle* means "one sent forth." Use the paper Apostles to model how these men spent time with the Lord and then received power from Him to go and help other people in differing areas.

MODERN APOSTLES: Because God loves us, He has given us prophets and apostles in our day to help bless us as well! They receive power and authority from Christ. On the back side of the paper Apostles, write the names of modern-day Apostles.

ME: We also have important things we can do to help in the Lord's work. Discuss specific ways we can access His power to help us in our lives and to help others who may be needing help. Cut out the "Me!" piece and have each person write on it one thing they will do to feel the Lord's power and love in their lives.

Testify of Christ's love for us and desire to help us.

EXTENSION

Attach the Apostles and "Me" pictures to separate paper strips and connect them all as paper chains in a circle around the Jesus picture to demonstrate how the Apostles as well as us can receive direct power from Jesus Christ. Discuss instances of when the Apostles might need to receive revelation to guide the Church (such as how to do baptisms) versus times when we might need to receive personal revelation for ourselves in our own lives.

Have everyone spend a few minutes using play dough to model one thing they would ask for if they could have anything they wanted. Let others guess what each creation is.

To simplify, have everyone draw a picture of what they would ask for instead of using play dough.

Funny Scriptures:

Read or summarize Luke 11:9–13. Then follow these directions to discuss how funny these verses are:

> Have the kids ask you for BREAD. Pretend to give them a ROCK instead of bread. Laugh about how silly that is.

Discuss: Would someone who loves you give you something bad if you asked for something good? Why not?

Would Heavenly Father give you something bad if you asked Him for something good? (No!) Why not? (Because He loves you!)

> Have the kids ask you for a FISH. Pretend to give them a SERPENT instead.

Does Heavenly Father always give us exactly what we ask for? Why are prayers sometimes answered differently than the way we expect?

> Have the kids ask you for an EGG. Pretend to give them a SCORPION instead.

Discuss how Heavenly Father and Jesus want to give us good things. If we ask Them for a giant 20-foot-tall stuffed animal that can magically turn things into candy, though, they probably won't give it to us because They know that it's not necessary for our eternal happiness.

THINGS I CAN PRAY FOR: Jesus taught that we shouldn't use "vain repetitions" when we pray (Matthew 6:7). How can we make sure the words we use when we pray are meaningful?

Cut out the "Prayer Cards" on the Week 11 Activity Sheet and place them in an upside-down pile. Take turns choosing one from the pile and following the directions on it. When all cards have been discussed, put them in order for when we would say that part in our prayers (Dear Heavenly Father, I Thank Thee, I Ask Thee, In the Name of Jesus Christ, Amen).

TESTIFY

Talk about how important prayers are. Share stories of times our prayers have been answered. Testify that our prayers are heard and that Heavenly Father and Jesus want to give us good things in our lives.

What are some of your favorite stories? Give the kids a chance to summarize some stories that they like. Explain that Jesus liked to use stories to teach things to people. He called these stories "parables." The parables He shared taught many different lessons.

Parable Booklet Story Time

Create a comfortable spot for some story time fun! Spread a blanket out on the floor, set out some milk and cookies, or anything else you can think of to create a cozy area!

Cut out the parable booklets from the Week 12 Activity Sheets. Hide them around the room, and let the kids take turns finding them. As each is found, read the scriptures for each parable, and then read and discuss the booklet for it.

There are many different levels to the lessons that can be learned from these parables, so don't feel limited to focusing only on what is in these booklets. Since there is so much information packed into these parables, it may be a good idea to choose a couple at a time to focus on instead of trying to cover every parable in one setting.

EXTENSION

If you choose to focus on "The Parable of the Sower," it is a great idea to actually plant a seed and talk about ways we can take care of it. After talking about how we can help seeds grow well (giving them good soil, watering them, being gentle with them, etc.), discuss ways we can help our testimonies grow (praying, studying the scriptures, etc.). Use the flower outline on the Week 12 Activity Sheet to have them write or draw specific ways we can nurture our testimonies on each of the flower petals.

Give everyone one minute to see how high they can count. How big is the number 5,000? Help them see that it's a pretty big number!

Fish and Bread

Set out two fish-shaped crackers or treats and five rolls. How many people do you think these could be split up between? Read, summarize, and discuss the story of the miracle of Christ feeding 5,000 hungry people found in Matthew 14:16–21, Mark 6:33–44, and John 6:5–14. Discuss how much food they started with, how many people were fed, and how much was left over.

CRAFT

Explain that each one of us is important to the Lord and has something we can offer to Him. Have each person color and cut out 5 loaves of bread and 2 fish from the Week 13 Activity Sheet. On the back of each loaf and fish, ask them to write something they might give up to the Lord (time to study Him, service to others, etc.). Have each of them create a basket using the Week 13 Activity Sheet and place their fish and bread inside of it. Use the baskets and bread/fish to retell the story. Remind them that whatever we are able to give Christ can be magnified into much more through His power.

TESTIFY

Discuss the following quote from Elder Jeffrey R. Holland: "Don't worry about Christ running out of ability to help you. His grace is sufficient. That is the spiritual, eternal lesson of the feeding of the 5,000" ("Come unto Me," *Ensign*, May 1998)." Testify of Christ's power, love, and ability to help us in our lives. Remind them that He will give us many blessings for small sacrifices that we make in our lives.

Discuss what we love about Easter! Remind them that even though the treats and the Easter egg hunts are fun, we celebrate Easter because of Christ's Resurrection.

Look at these pictures of Jesus Christ in Gethsemane, on the cross, and after being resurrected. Discuss what we know about each one and what they have to do with Easter.

Read and discuss 1 Peter 1:3–11. Testify that Christ lived on Earth, suffered in Gethsemane and on the cross for us, and that He was resurrected and still lives and helps us in our lives.

TREAT

Follow instructions on the Week 14 Activity Sheet for making "Christ Is Risen Rolls."

game: Who Am I?

Cut apart the pieces on the Week 15 Activity Sheet. Keep the Jesus card out, but place all of the others in a bag. Take turns pulling one out of the bag and giving clues about who that person is until others can guess it correctly. Give the "Jesus" card to the last person. After the others have guessed who it is, discuss who He is to us.

Read and discuss Matthew 16:13–17. Pay attention to how Peter responded to Christ's question to him ("Whom say ye that I am?"). Have them practice saying, "Thou are the Christ, the Son of the living God" (Matthew 16:16). Break this response down and talk about what it means. How can we also know for ourselves that He is the Christ, the Son of the living God?

Review the things we've learned about Jesus Christ. What stories can we remember that we've learned about Him?

SONG/TESTIMONIES

Give everyone a circle cutout picture of Jesus from the Week 15 Activity Sheet. Have them hold this while listening to a song about Jesus, such as "I Believe in Christ." Tell them to pay attention to how they feel as they think about Him. Who is He to us and what does His life mean to us?

Take turns sharing testimonies and sharing how we would answer if Jesus asked us, "Whom say ye that I am?" (Matthew 16:15).

EXTENSION

Older kids can write their answers to who Christ is to them on the back of their pictures of Jesus. Then have everyone pass their pictures around and read what everyone else wrote.

Take a minute to talk about neighbors. What are your neighbors like? Who are they? Explain that Jesus taught that everyone is our neighbor, even people who don't live close to us, people who are different from us, and people who are unkind to us.

The Good Samaritan

To help us understand who our neighbors are, Jesus told a story about a Samaritan. In those times, there were two groups of people who didn't usually get along very well: the Jews and the Samaritans.

- Cut out the good Samaritan story figures from the Week 16 Activity Sheet.

- Show the picture of the wounded Jewish man and explain that he was robbed and almost killed by thieves.

- Show the pictures of the Jewish priest, Jewish Levite, and Samaritan. All three of these men happened to come across the injured man. Ask which of these three people they think was most likely to stop and help the man.

- Use the story figures to act out the story of the good Samaritan while reading Luke 10:30–37.

- How is Christ like a good Samaritan to us?

- How can we be like good Samaritans to others around us?

Role-Play Scenarios

Cut out the scenario slips from the Week 16 Activity Sheet. Take turns choosing one from a pile and role-playing how we could respond like a good Samaritan would.

DISCUSS

President Howard W. Hunter taught, "We need to remember that though we make our friends, God has made our neighbors—everywhere. Love should have no boundary; we should have no narrow loyalties" ("The Lord's Touchstone," *Ensign*, Nov. 1986).

Testify of Heavenly Father and Christ's love for each of us. Encourage everyone to try to love and serve others as Christ does.

EXTENSION

The kids can wear the story figures as necklaces while retelling the story of the good Samaritan and pretending to be the characters in the story.

WEEK 17
JOHN 10

Sheep in the Fold

Explain that a "fold" is a large enclosure where sheep can be kept safe at night. A fold usually has stone walls and one opening. Set out the fold enclosure picture from the Week 17 Activity Sheet. Let the kids use blocks to build a wall along the outlined edge of the fold. While building, discuss how the gospel of Jesus Christ keeps us safe from spiritual dangers.

WOLF: If a wolf comes close to the sheep, would a good shepherd run away or stay there and protect the sheep? Explain that a shepherd who truly cared would do anything to save his sheep.

THE GOOD SHEPHERD: Read and discuss John 10:11–15. Who is the Good Shepherd (Jesus Christ)? Discuss how much He loves every one of us, and that is why He suffered in Gethsemane and gave His life for us on the cross.

SHEEP: "He that will hear my voice shall be my sheep" (Mosiah 26:21). Discuss ways we can hear Christ's voice (through the scriptures, words of Church leaders, personal revelation, etc.). Read and discuss John 10:27–29.

Hide the sheep from the Week 17 Activity Sheet around the room. Everyone will take turns finding one. Once they've found one, they will answer that question and then put that sheep safely inside the fold to represent how listening to Christ and obeying His gospel keeps us safe.

Read John 10:1–18 while using the paper sheep, wolf, and shepherd pieces to act out what each verse is describing.

Testify of Christ's love for us and the blessings we receive for listening to and following Him.

EXTENSION

- Have everyone write their name on a sheep. John 10:3 says that Jesus "calleth his own sheep by name." Testify that He knows each of us personally by name.

- Discuss the "other sheep" Jesus described in John 10:16. Read who He was referring to in 3 Nephi 15:21–16:5.

- Write specific commandments on the walls of the fold and explain how they might keep our spirits safe.

Tell everyone you're going to give them a bag of ten things. Chocolate gold coins would work well for this, but you could use any treat or other fun items. Either give each kid their own bag or set out one bag for them all to share. Make sure each bag only has nine items in it instead of ten. Help them realize that there are only nine in the bag and one is missing. Is the last item worth looking for? For this week's activity, we will do some work to find the missing coin (or whatever other item you put in the bags)!

PARABLES: In Luke 15, Christ shared three parables. These parables were about a lost sheep, a lost coin, and a prodigal son. Summarize each parable as described in this chapter, and have the kids take turns retelling the stories or acting them out. What was lost in each story? How was it found? How did people feel when the item was found?

HEADS OR TAILS: Cut out the coins on the Week 18 Activity Sheets. Put the "Tail Question Coins" upside down in a pile. Put strings through the "Head Coin Necklaces" and place them in a different area. Take turns flipping a real coin. If it lands on tails, they will take one of the question coins out of the pile, read it, and discuss it. If it lands on heads, that person will grab one of the "Head Coin Necklaces" and put it on the person who is sitting closest to them who does not yet have a necklace. Continue until all of the question coins have been discussed. Once everyone has their coin necklace, if additional coins land on the head side, whoever flipped the coin will give a compliment to the person closest to them instead of giving them a necklace.*

WE ARE VALUABLE: Give everyone their tenth chocolate coin to add to their bags. Explain that Christ's parables teach us that each of us is like the lost sheep, the lost coin, or the prodigal son. At different times and for different reasons in our lives, we might become more distanced from God. Because we are valuable to Him, He sent His Son to pave a way for us to make our way back to Him again. How can we turn back toward Christ when we feel ourselves drifting away from Him? How can we help others draw nearer to Him as well?

Testify that Christ notices when even just one out of many people is lost, and He rejoices when they are found.

*Idea from Lucy Schoneman

In Mark 10:17, a man asked Jesus, "Good Master, what shall I do that I may inherit eternal life?" Listen to what Jesus told him to do and how he responded in Matthew 19:16–22, Mark 10:17–22, or Luke 18:18–23.

The Candy Sacrifice Game

Explain that sometimes the Lord asks us to make sacrifices in our lives. Follow the instructions on the Week 19 Activity Sheet to play "The Candy Sacrifice Game" while discussing some of the sacrifices we might make. Warn them beforehand that they will be asked to make sacrifices in this game, just like the rich young man was asked to make sacrifices in Matthew 19. We get to choose if we make those sacrifices or not, and they're not always easy to make, but we know that we will be richly blessed when we choose to do those difficult things.

Note: The winner of this game is whoever has the LEAST amount of candies left at the end, since that means they made the most sacrifices. Make sure they know not to eat any candies until the end of the game as well. To illustrate the idea that we receive more blessings when we make more sacrifices, you might want to give bigger prizes to the top winners or to players who chose to make sacrifices each time they were asked to. Don't tell them beforehand what the prize will be! After giving them their prizes, emphasize that the rewards we will receive from Christ for sacrifices that we make will be much greater than any type of candy or other worldly prizes.

CHALLENGE

Discuss the following exercise suggested by Larry R. Lawrence and invite everyone to try it out on their own. Testify of the blessings we receive when we ask for the Lord's guidance and help in our progression, and then when we follow through with any sacrifices He asks us to make.

"I would like to suggest that each of you participate in a spiritual exercise sometime soon, perhaps even tonight while saying your prayers. Humbly ask the Lord the following question: 'What is keeping me from progressing?' In other words: 'What lack I yet?' Then wait quietly for a response. If you are sincere, the answer will soon become clear. It will be revelation intended just for you.

"Perhaps the Spirit will tell you that you need to forgive someone. Or you may receive a message to be more selective about the movies you watch or the music you listen to. You may feel impressed to be more honest in your business dealings or more generous in your fast offerings. The possibilities are endless." (Larry R. Lawrence, "What Lack I Yet?," Ensign, Nov. 2015)

Heart Sort

Some of the rulers of the Jews believed in Jesus but would not tell other people that they believed in Him. John 12:42–43 states, "Nevertheless among the chief rulers also many believed on him; but because of the Pharisees they did not confess him, lest they should be put out of the synagogue: For they loved the praise of men more than the praise of God."

What does it mean to love the praise of men more than the praise of God?

Did these people care more about what other people thought about them or what God thought about them?

Role-play how we could react if others were making fun of us for our belief in Christ.

Role-play how we can also show respect to others who are sharing their religious beliefs with us.

Loving God and Others as Myself: What are the greatest commandments? Read Matthew 22:34–40. What are specific ways we can show that we love God and others as ourselves? What does it mean to love God with our whole heart, soul, and mind? If we truly love God, we will also be kind and loving to the people around us.

Heart Activity

Cut out the pieces on the Week 20 Activity Sheet. Sort the pieces into two groups based on which actions show love toward God and others and which do not. Glue the pieces that show love onto the heart. Throw the other pieces away.

Testify that God loves us all a lot. Encourage everyone to find ways to show their love for God and others.

If possible, go sit outside underneath a deciduous tree that loses its leaves in the autumn. Discuss what we'd expect to see happen to its leaves during different seasons of the year. When does it start to lose its leaves? When do they grow back? If it's a fruit tree, when does the fruit start to grow on it?

Leaf Tracing/Signs of the Second Coming

Give everyone a piece of paper and pencils or crayons that they can use to trace leaves or do a leaf-rubbing with. Jesus shared a parable about trees to help teach about the timing of when He would come to the earth again (His Second Coming). In Luke 21:29–31, Mark 13:28–31, and Matthew 24:32–33 (also explained in Joseph Smith—Matthew 1:38–40), He taught that just like we know summer is getting closer when we see leaves growing back on trees, we can know that the Second Coming of Jesus Christ is getting closer when we see certain signs. He hasn't told us the exact day and time when He will return to the earth, but He wants us to be watching for the signs so we can be ready to be with Him again.

Read, discuss, and summarize some of the signs we've been told to watch for in Mark 13:21–27, Luke 21:25–28, and Joseph Smith—Matthew 1:21–37. On their leaf drawings, everyone will write or draw some of the signs we've been given to help us know the Second Coming is near. Discuss ways we can spiritually prepare ourselves for the Savior's Second Coming.

I Can Prepare

Cut out the pieces on the Week 21 Activity Sheet. Place the "I Can Prepare for the Second Coming of Jesus Christ" picture on a wall in the room. Put the "Preparation Sorting Cards" in a bag and take turns choosing one without looking. If the card that is chosen is an action that would strengthen your testimony and help you be spiritually prepared for the Second Coming, everyone will go stand by the wall that has the picture of Jesus on it. If it's not something that would help prepare you to see Christ again, everyone will go to the opposite side of the room. Continue until all of the cards have been drawn out of the bag.

TESTIFY

Explain that the Second Coming of the Savior will be a happy time. We will get to walk and talk with Jesus, and there will be no more evil on Earth. Encourage everyone to choose one thing they will do this week to prepare for His Second Coming.

This lesson focuses on some sacred topics. To help set a reverent vibe, start by explaining what the Last Supper was (the final meal Christ would have on Earth with His disciples before His Crucifixion). Matthew 26:30 teaches that at the Last Supper, the Savior and His disciples sang a hymn. Talk about what it might have felt like to be there. Choose some hymns to reverently sing. Share what Jesus Christ means to us, and remind them that He willingly suffered for us because He loves us.

Picture Walk

The New Testament describes many important events that happened in the last days of the life of Christ. We will learn about some of these events by doing a "Picture Walk" for this week's activity. Set the "Picture Walk" pictures up in different areas. Walk to each station in order, read the corresponding scriptures, and discuss them one at a time.

Bookmarks

To help keep the kids' attention while doing this activity, give them each a blank bookmark from the Week 22 Activity Sheet. As they go to each station, they will either draw a small picture or write a brief summary of each story. If they are old enough, after the last station, you can play reverent music while they silently write their testimonies of Christ on the back of their bookmark. It could also be a good idea to laminate these for them.

TESTIMONIES: After doing the "Picture Walk," give everyone a chance to share summaries of one of the stations that was meaningful to them and share testimonies of Christ.

EXTENSION

While talking about Christ instituting the sacrament, you could set out some flat bread to share with everyone. While eating, discuss ways we can remember Christ as we partake of the sacrament in the future.

Read John 13:33–35 and discuss why loving others shows that we truly believe in Jesus and are His disciples.

Read and discuss the following words of Christ. Remind them of how much both Heavenly Father and Jesus Christ love us.

> "As the Father hath loved me, so have I loved you." *John 15:9*

> "Greater love hath no man than this, that a man lay down his life for his friends." *John 15:13*

Heavenly Father gave us the incredible gift of His Son, Jesus Christ. Because They both love us lots, Jesus gave His life for us, His friends.

Because Jesus loves us, He wanted us to be able to feel His presence even after His death on the cross. Jesus told His disciples that after He left, He would send them the Holy Ghost to help them so that they would not be left alone. The Holy Ghost is not something that we can see with our eyes, but the influence of the Holy Ghost can be powerful in our lives. How does the Holy Ghost help us? Read and discuss John 14:16–17, John 14:26–27, John 15:26, John 16:7–11, and John 16:13–14.

Discuss this quote from James E. Faust:

> "The Holy Ghost bears witness of the truth and impresses upon the soul the reality of God the Father and the Son Jesus Christ so deeply that no earthly power or authority can separate him from that knowledge." ("The Gift of the Holy Ghost—A Sure Compass," May 1989 Ensign)

The Holy Ghost

Assemble the gift box on the Week 23 Activity Sheet to represent the gift of the Holy Ghost. Cut out the "Holy Ghost Description Hearts." Read the scriptures written on the gift box one at a time. With each scripture verse, have them listen carefully for the words "teach," "guide," or "testify." They will then tape the correct Holy Ghost description heart onto the corresponding scripture heart on the gift box.

Remind them that the Holy Ghost is something that abides with us, dwells with us, and is inside of us (John 14:16–17). Place a battery-powered tea light inside of the gift box to represent the Holy Ghost inside of us. Sit in a dark area with the gift box and tea light.

Share examples of times when we've felt the influence of the Holy Ghost in our lives. Discuss how precious the gift of the Holy Ghost is. What actions can we take to bring the influence of the Holy Ghost into our lives? Remind them that the Holy Ghost can guide, comfort, warn, teach, and testify of truth to us. Testify that the Holy Ghost can help us feel closer to Jesus Christ and bring more light into our lives.

GETHSEMANE: Sing "Gethsemane" by Melanie Hoffman (hoffmanhouse.com). Review what happened in the Garden of Gethsemane. Read and discuss Luke 22:39–46. Remind them that Jesus suffered in Gethsemane for us because He loves us. He felt every kind of sadness and hurt that we will ever feel. Because of that, He can help us through any kind of sadness or pain we might experience.

Sad Face

Tape the sad face from the Week 24 Activity Sheet onto the wall without showing the back side. Let everyone write or draw things that might make them feel sad or hurt around the face. After it's full, turn the picture over to show Jesus on the other side. Explain that Jesus has felt these things too. Because He has felt them, He knows how to help us feel better when we're going through them.

ANGEL: Who supported and strengthened Jesus Christ while He was suffering in Gethsemane? Read Luke 22:42–44 and discuss how an angel strengthened Him.

Do angels strengthen us in our lives as well? Discuss how angels can be heavenly angels that we don't see, but often they are other people around us who help and support us. How can we support others as they go through hard times? Discuss specific Christlike actions we can take to be earthly angels who support and strengthen those around us.

Angel Card

Give each person an angel card from the Week 24 Activity Sheet. Encourage them to put it somewhere where it will remind them that:

Heavenly, unseen angels can support and strengthen us in our lives.	*Friends, family, and others around us can be like angels as they support and strengthen us.*	*We can be like angels as we support and strengthen others around us.*

Testify that Jesus loves and cares for us. He can help us because He has felt everything we might go through. It's important for us to also try to help those around us.

EXTENSION

If you are teaching older kids, you could have them write a note to thank someone who has been like an angel to them in their life.

Look at the pictures of Christ's trial and Crucifixion on this page. Take turns sharing what we know about Jesus's death. Remind them that on the third day, Jesus came back to life (He was resurrected).

Matching Activity

Cut apart the squares on the Week 25 Activity Sheet. Arrange them in an upside-down array and take turns trying to find matches. As each match is found, read and discuss the corresponding scripture verses.

Once all matches have been found, place the pictures in order and summarize what happened. Set them around a picture of Christ.

Share our feelings for Christ and what He went through for us. Remind them that Christ taught, "If ye love me, keep my commandments" (John 14:15). Discuss how keeping the commandments shows our love for Christ.

Testify of Heavenly Father and Jesus Christ's love for us. Their love was the reason Jesus went through so much pain and suffering for us (in Gethsemane as well as on the cross). Remind them that because of the Atonement of Jesus Christ, we will be resurrected, and we can be forgiven of our sins.

Word Scramble

Cut apart the words on the Week 26 Activity Sheet and mix them up. Give the kids time to try to unscramble them. Give them hints as needed. (It starts with the word "He." It's what an angel told women who were looking for Jesus's body in the tomb, etc.) Once they've figured out the phrase "He is not here: for he is risen," practice saying it out loud together. Mix the words up again, race to see how fast they can unscramble them, and see if they can memorize the phrase. Discuss why these words are so important and how they can give us hope.

The Resurrection of Jesus Christ

Cut out the images of Jesus labeled "spirit" and "body" from the Week 26 Activity Sheet. Hold them together while explaining that all of us have a body as well as a spirit. Our spirits are what make it possible for our bodies to move, talk, sing, and so on. Review some of the things Jesus did while He was alive and act them out with the paper Jesus pieces (calming a storm, feeding 5,000 people, etc.). Explain that after He died, His spirit and body were separated. His body was placed in a tomb. Use the paper pieces and tomb picture from the Week 26 Activity Sheets to model this. Discuss what happens to our spirits when we die.

Read, discuss, and summarize John 20:1–18, Matthew 28:1–10, Mark 16:1–14, or Luke 24:1–48. Use the labeled images of Jesus to model how Christ's body and spirit were reunited when He was resurrected. Discuss how we will all be resurrected after death because of Christ's victory over death. Our bodies and spirits will never again be separated.

THOMAS: Read, discuss, and summarize the story of Thomas having a hard time believing others who said that Christ had risen again (John 20:19–29). Thomas said that he would only believe if he also got to see and feel the nail prints in Jesus's hands and feet. John 20:29 states, "Blessed are they that have not seen, and yet have believed." How can we believe in Christ even if we don't see Him right now? Why is that difficult to do sometimes? What actions can we take to help us feel His presence in our lives?

Testify that Jesus Christ lives. He was resurrected, and even though we might not see Him right now, He is aware of us and loves each of us.

EXTENSION

Read Doctrine and Covenants 138 to learn about what Jesus's spirit was doing while His body was in the tomb.

PETER: For 40 days after His Resurrection, Jesus visited and taught His disciples. He then ascended into heaven and promised to return again in the latter days "in like manner" (Acts 1:11). After Jesus Christ ascended to His Father, Peter became the one in charge of leading Christ's Church and teaching others about Jesus Christ and His gospel. Peter was powerful in his testimony of Christ and performed many great miracles in His name. Read and discuss the miracle performed in Acts 3:1–8. After this, when others commanded him not to speak about Jesus and threatened to put him in jail if he did, Peter (as well as John) responded, "We cannot but speak the things which we have seen and heard" (Acts 4:20). They continued to give bold testimonies of Christ.

When we follow the teachings of Christ, they can change us. How do Peter's actions in Acts 1–5 show that he had changed from the night when he denied Christ three times?

ANANIAS AND SAPPHIRA: How are we changed when we do not follow the teachings of Christ and the people He has called to help spread His work? Read, summarize, and discuss the story of Ananias and Sapphira being dishonest in Acts 5:1–11. Is being honest an important thing to the Lord? (Yes!) Clarify that we won't die when we're dishonest, but this story helps us understand how important honesty is to Heavenly Father.

Discuss the following quote:

"In our time those found in dishonesty do not die as did Ananias and Sapphira, but something within them dies. Conscience chokes, character withers, self-respect vanishes, integrity dies . . . We cannot be less than honest, we cannot be less than true, we cannot be less than virtuous if we are to keep sacred the trust given us." (President Gordon B. Hinckley, "We Believe in Being Honest," Ensign, Nov. 1990)

Honest Oscar Activity

Cut out the Honest Oscar and Dishonest Darius finger puppets from the Week 27 Activity Sheet. Assign one person to be Oscar and another to be Darius. Children will place their fingers through the finger holes in the bottom. Give situations for them to act out. Whoever is Oscar will act out an example of an honest response. Whoever is Darius will act out a dishonest response for that situation. Discuss the blessings of being honest.

Testify that Heavenly Father and Jesus Christ love us no matter what. They will help us as we strive to be more honest and Christlike in our lives.

STEPHEN: When the Jewish leaders rejected the Savior and those who taught about Him, Stephen said to them, "Ye do always resist the Holy Ghost" (Acts 7:51). What does it mean to resist the Holy Ghost? In contrast, Stephen was "full of the Holy Ghost" (Acts 7:55). How do we feel when we are full of the Holy Ghost?

Cup Activity

Tape the "Resisting the Holy Ghost" and "Accepting the Holy Ghost" labels from the Week 28 Activity Sheet onto two separate cups. Cut out the sorting cards and place them upside down in a pile. Take turns choosing one out of the pile. Decide if the card describes a circumstance of resisting the Holy Ghost or listening to the Holy Ghost's promptings. Place the card in the corresponding cup.

STORIES

Share the stories of the following people found in the Bible. Decide if each person accepted or rejected the influence of the Holy Ghost in their decisions described in the verses:

People in synagogues who opposed Stephen (Acts 6:8–14)	Philip and the Ethiopian Man (Acts 8:26–39)	Saul (Acts 9:1–20)	Tabitha (Acts 9:36–42)

DISCUSS

Stephen was so full of the Holy Ghost that he was even willing to die for his belief in Christ and testimony of Him. How can we feel the Holy Ghost more strongly in our own lives? What would we be willing to do to defend our testimonies of Jesus?

Christ Scramble

Cut out the letters to spell "CHRIST" from the Week 29 Activity Sheet. Mix them up and have the kids unscramble them. Review specific reasons why Christ is important to us.

CHRISTIAN: Read Acts 11:26. Explain that anyone who believes in and follows Jesus Christ is called a Christian. Do you believe in Christ? If so, you are a Christian! Add the letters "I-A-N" to the end of the "CHRIST" word that was made in the scramble activity. Help them see how the word "Christian" is based off of the word "Christ."

Circle Activity

Tape the "CHRISTIAN" letters onto a separate piece of paper. Sit in a circle and pass the paper around. When each person gets the paper, they will say one way a person might act if they are a true follower of Christ. What types of things might we do and say if we are truly Christlike?

Button Activity

Cut out the "Christian" and "Not Christlike" buttons from the Week 29 Activity Sheet. Tape them up on opposite sides of the room. Say different scenarios out loud, and after you've said them, have the kids run to the side of the room to push the "button" corresponding to whether or not those actions are things Christ would do.

Testify that we will all fall short of being Christlike at times in our lives. Remind them that part of being a Christian is that we repent when we recognize our shortcomings. Remind them of the blessings we receive from striving to follow Christ and become like Him and the help that He will give us as we do so.

EXTENSION

Research what your given first and/or last name means. Why are names important? What does it mean to take upon yourself the name of Jesus Christ or to be a Christian?

HAPPY: What kinds of things make you happy? Spend a couple of minutes talking about anything that makes us happy, whether it's ice cream, songs, amusement parks, etc.

Candy Sharing

Set out a treat that you enjoy (make sure there's enough to share with everyone). Explain why you enjoy it. Tell them that since you also want them to be happy, you brought some to share. Let everyone eat it and talk about how great it is to share with others. Jesus taught, "It is more blessed to give than to receive" (Acts 20:35). Discuss what this means.

GOSPEL SHARING: Something that's even more important than candy is the gospel of Jesus Christ. Because Paul knew how good the gospel was, he went on many missionary journeys and traveled thousands of miles to share the gospel with as many people as he could! He even shared it in prison! Act out the story of Paul and Silas sharing the gospel in prison (Acts 16:25–33).

Give everyone a minute to share something they know about the gospel that is important to them. How would they explain their beliefs to someone who didn't know anything about them?

THINGS PAUL TAUGHT: Cut out the puzzle pieces from the Week 30 Activity Sheet. Each piece includes a truth that Paul taught during his missionary travels. Take turns choosing a puzzle piece, reading what's on the piece, and discussing what it means. Arrange the pieces to show the picture on the back. Discuss what it means to be the "offspring of God" (Acts 17:29). How does it feel to know that we are His children?

DISCUSS: How can we be both humble and bold like Paul as we share the truths of the gospel that we know? How can the spirit guide us in our efforts?

Testify that we are children of God, and that He loves each of us. He wants us to be close to Him, and He wants us to help others learn more about Him.

EXTENSION

Share the gospel like Paul did, but through song! Record a video of yourself singing, "I Am a Child of God," or another song about Heavenly Father and Jesus. Send the video to at least one other person and encourage them to keep the string going by recording a video of themselves singing the same song and passing it on to someone else.*

If teaching older kids, let each one choose one place Paul shared the gospel, read the scripture verses for that place, and share a summary from that section with everyone else. If possible, find a map showing the places he served.

Thessalonica	Berea	Athens	Corinth	Ephesus	Caesarea, Antioch, Galatia, Phrygia
Acts 17:1–4	(Acts 17:10–12)	(Acts 17:16–31)	(Acts 18:1–6)	(Acts 18:19–21)	(Acts 18:22–23)

*Idea from Hannah Schoneman

TRUE/FALSE QUIZ:

If bad things happen in my life, that means God hates me. (False)	God can be with me through hard times in my life. (True)	Paul's life was easy and painless after he changed and decided to follow the Lord. (False)	God loves me and wants to help me. (True)

Review how Paul used to be called Saul. He was mean to people in the Lord's Church, but one day he had a vision that made him decide to repent and change. Summarize the story of Paul's conversion (Acts 22). He still went through some difficult times after he decided to follow Christ, but he knew that the Lord was with him. We're going to learn three stories about things that happened to Paul after he started believing and following Jesus Christ and His gospel.

Puppet Theater

Follow the directions found on the Week 31 Activity Sheet to make a puppet theater box. Cut out the figures and attach them to sticks. Use the stick puppets to reenact the following stories while reading the scripture verses for each:

STORY 1 Paul in Prison—Explain that when it says he was taken into the castle, that means he was cast into prison in the castle. (Acts 23:10–11)	**STORY 2** Paul on the Ship (Acts 27:18–26)	**STORY 3** Paul with the Snake (Acts 28:1–6)

While listening and acting out the stories, assign one person to be in charge of the "Heavenly Father and Jesus Are with Us During Hard Times" sign. As soon as they hear something in the verses that shows that the Lord was with Paul through these difficult experiences, they will hold that sign up.

Note: To simplify, skip making the theater box and just use the paper figures how they are.

DISCUSS: In what ways does the Lord help us? Explain that He might not take away hard things that we go through, but He'll help us as we go through them. What are some difficult times we have gone through or might go through? How have we or how can we feel the Lord's presence as we go through these times?

Testify that Heavenly Father and Jesus are aware of us at all times in our lives. They might not take away our trials, but They will help us through them in the ways that They know are best.

Cut out the target picture from the Week 32 Activity Sheet. Remind them that our goal in life is to become like Heavenly Father and Jesus and return to be with Them again. That's what the bullseye in the middle of the target represents.

Give everyone some time to make paper airplanes (or, to simplify, crumple up a small piece of paper). Set the target on the floor a long distance away from where you will be throwing from. The farther away the target is, the better this activity will work. You don't want to make it too easy for them to hit the bullseye on their own! Take turns throwing airplanes/papers at the target and see how often they can hit right on the bullseye with the tip of their airplane pointing directly to God.

ALL HAVE SINNED AND FALLEN SHORT: Afterward, ask if anyone hit the bullseye every single time. Compare this to the scripture that says, "For all have sinned, and come short of the glory of God" (Romans 3:23). None of us live perfect lives, just like nobody hit the bullseye every time. We all sin and fall short of being perfect like God. Does God want to help us hit our spiritual "bullseye"? (Yes.) How does He help us? (Through Jesus Christ.) Give everyone one more turn to throw their airplane. This time have one person represent Jesus. That person will pick up each person's airplane wherever it landed and move it to be right on the bullseye.

JESUS CHRIST: Explain that it's important to do all of the good things we can, but our good works aren't enough to earn our way to heaven. The sacrifice that Jesus Christ made for us is what makes it possible for us to hit the "bullseye" and be with God again. Romans 1:17 tells us we should "live by faith." Does that mean we say we believe in Jesus but then do nothing about it? (No.) If we really believe in and love Jesus, we will do our best to follow His teachings, even if our best is imperfect. Discuss some of His teachings we need to follow (getting baptized, loving others, keeping the Sabbath Day holy, etc.).

Badges

Romans 1:16 states, "For I am not ashamed of the gospel of Christ: for it is the power of God unto salvation to every one that believeth." Talk about what that means. Give everyone a badge from the Week 32 Activity Sheet to color. While they are coloring it, discuss how we can live our lives in ways that show we're grateful for Jesus Christ and His gospel rather than being ashamed of Him.

Testify of Jesus Christ's important role in our lives. Remind them that Heavenly Father and Jesus love each of us, and that is why they sent Jesus to help us.

EXTENSION

Read and discuss the talk "The Gift of Grace" by Dieter F. Uchtdorf (*Ensign*, May 2015).

Try to Erase God's Love

On a rock, use permanent marker to write the words "God's Love." Set out an eraser and let each kid take turns trying to erase the words. Explain that just like the words on this rock can't be erased, nothing can take God's love away from us. Take turns hiding the rock and letting others try to find it. Discuss how there might be times in our lives when we're not sure if God still loves us or we might not even be thinking about Him. Just like the rock, His love is always there and real, even when we might not see or notice it. He is always aware of us and full of love for us.

Note: You can also write the words on a piece of paper instead of a rock, though it may get ripped as they try to erase the words.

Read and discuss Romans 8:35–39. Share stories of times we've felt God's love in our lives. Does He love us during good times and bad times? Does He love us when we make good choices? Does He love us when we make mistakes? How does that love help guide our actions? Practice saying and memorizing the phrase, "[Nothing] shall be able to separate us from the love of God!"

Nothing Can Separate Me From the Love of God

You will need to get some strips of construction paper for this craft.

Give each person a set of hearts from the Week 33 Activity Sheet. Let them draw a picture of themselves on the "Nothing Can Separate Me . . ." piece. Have them cut out the hearts. Fold strips of construction paper like an accordion between the hearts. Draw pictures on the accordion strip of times you've felt God's love or things you see in the world around you that help you know He loves you. Use the accordion strip to connect the two hearts together.

Testify that God is real and loves us always. That doesn't mean that the choices we make don't matter. It means that He understands that each of us has weaknesses and that He can help us "overcome evil with good" (Romans 12:21).

EXTENSION

Get heart-shaped pieces of wood from a craft store, or cut them out of cardboard or cardstock. Let each kid decorate one with the words "God's Love" and glue/Mod-Podge a picture of themselves onto it to remind them that God's love is always with them.

1 Corinthians 1:23–25 tells us that some people thought Paul's teachings were foolish, but Paul taught that our "faith should not stand in the wisdom of men, but in the power of God" (1 Corinthians 2:5). If people tell us we're foolish for our beliefs, how can we know if we should believe them or not? Discuss ways we can rely on the Lord to tell us truths rather than relying on other people's wisdom. Why is it difficult sometimes to trust more in the wisdom of God than in what other people might tell us?

Role-play ways we can respond when people teach things that contradict God's wisdom. Give specific scenarios and help them think of ways they can remain loving and humble while being bold and remembering to rely on the Lord's wisdom at the same time.

THE HOLY GHOST: How does the Holy Ghost help convey messages of truth to us from God? Remind them that the Holy Ghost is a great gift we have from God to help us in this life. Review some of the things the Holy Ghost can do for us (guide us, comfort us, testify of truths to us, etc.). Read and discuss 1 Corinthians 2:11–14.

OUR BODIES ARE SACRED: How does the way we treat our bodies affect the Holy Ghost's ability to speak truths to us? Read 1 Corinthians 6:19–20 and discuss what it means when it says, "Your body is the temple of the Holy Ghost which is in you." Explain that the Holy Ghost is inside of us, and when we take good care of our bodies, it helps the Holy Ghost give us more light and wisdom from God.

Sorting Activity

Cut out the pieces from the Week 34 Activity Sheet and assemble the body and garbage containers. Bring their attention to the scripture written inside of the body container and remind them that the Holy Ghost dwells inside of us. What kind of place would the Holy Ghost want to be in? Place the word strips in an upside-down pile and take turns choosing one out of the pile. If the strip says something that will help our bodies and spirits be healthy and strong, place it in the body container. If it's something that wouldn't be good for us, place it in the garbage.

Encourage everyone to choose one thing they will do to help their bodies be better temples for the Holy Ghost this week. Testify that the help they will be capable of receiving from the Holy Ghost will grow as they take good care of their bodies.

EXTENSION

1 Corinthians 6:13–20 also mentions sexual immorality. Have an age-appropriate discussion on how living a chaste life also strengthens the light and power we can feel from the Holy Ghost. Read, discuss, or summarize the talk titled, "Love and Marriage," by Wendy W. Nelson (www.churchofjesuschrist.org/broadcasts/article/worldwide-devotionals/2017/01/love-and-marriage?lang=eng.).

SPIRITUAL GIFTS: Read through the spiritual gifts listed in 1 Corinthians 12:4–10. Explain that there are many other gifts we might have. Take some time to share specific things that you've noticed each person is good at (caring for others, saying heartfelt prayers, being a good listener, being good at speaking, remembering things well, etc.). Remind them that the things we do well are gifts that we have been given from God. We shouldn't use them to make others feel bad, but instead we should use them to help others.

Charity Heart Bouquet

1 Corinthians 13 explains that the most important gift we can receive is the gift of charity. Cut out the hearts from the Week 35 Activity Sheet. Attach them to skewer sticks or tooth picks. Let kids take turns choosing one without looking. As it is chosen, read the front description of what charity is. Then have them do the role-play scenario on the back of the heart to show how they can apply that aspect of charity in their lives. Place the hearts in a cup or vase after they've been discussed and display the charity heart bouquet somewhere to remind them of what charity is.

> *Tip: To show the words on each heart a little better, stick the skewer stick stems into a Styrofoam block or sphere inside of a pot or a vase with a large opening.*

> *To simplify, read what's on the hearts and do the role plays without turning them into a heart bouquet.*

Testify that Christ is the only one who has lived in a way that shows perfect charity. When we pray and ask for help gaining charity, He can fill us with this love.

EXTENSIONS

Write notes and make treats to share with others to let them know you love them!

Add paper hearts to the bouquet throughout the week each time someone does something that shows charity. Have them color a picture of what they did on each heart.

SONG: Review the story of Jesus Christ's Resurrection. Sing "Christ the Lord Is Risen Today" and discuss the words to it. Explain that the word *alleluia* means we're praising the Lord because we're happy! Why does Christ's Resurrection make us feel happy? Remind them that because Christ was resurrected, we will all be resurrected as well. The Apostle Paul was able to see Jesus Christ after He was resurrected, so he was able to teach about the reality of Christ's Resurrection in a powerful way. Read, discuss, and summarize 1 Corinthians 15:12–22. We will study more of his teachings in this week's activity.

Scripture Matching Game

Cut out the sun pieces from the Week 36 Activity Sheet. Place the sun rays upside down and take turns flipping two sun rays over to try to find matches. To make a match, they will need to find the scripture and the missing word that belongs to that scripture. Look up each scripture reference as needed to figure out which word matches the blank. Once each match is found, discuss what it means and let them glue the rays onto the sun circle.

PICTURES/STORIES: If possible, share pictures and stories of people you know who have passed away. What happened to them after they passed away? Review how we each have a spirit as well as a body. Discuss how the spirit and body separate at death. Will they stay separated forever? (No.) Remind them that because Jesus Christ was resurrected, we will also be resurrected. When we are resurrected, our spirits and bodies will join together again and our bodies will become immortal, which means they won't be able to die anymore (1 Corinthians 15:51–54).

SUN PICTURE: 1 Corinthians 15:40–41 teaches about the sun, moon, and stars. The sun represents being able to live with Heavenly Father again after we're resurrected. Let everyone draw pictures of themselves on the sun piece from the Week 36 Activity Sheet while talking about things we might need to do in this life to help us take steps toward living with God again.

Testify that because of Christ, we will all be resurrected after we die, and that those we love who have passed away are not gone forever.

EXTENSIONS

Talk about the different kingdoms of glory taught by Paul in 1 Corinthians 15:40–41. Further teachings on these kingdoms can be found in Doctrine and Covenants 76.

Discuss baptisms for the dead (mentioned in 1 Corinthians 15:29). Use stuffed animals to act out how vicarious baptisms for the dead help people who were not baptized during their time on Earth. Study Doctrine and Covenants 138:11–37 for more details on this.

Research names of ancestors who might need baptisms done for them.

GODLY SORROW: Have you ever felt bad or sad about something? Explain what the word *sorrow* means. Paul talked about the phrase "godly sorrow" (2 Corinthians 7:10). What do you think this means? Remind them that we all make mistakes! God knows we're not perfect, and that's why He sent us a Savior to make repentance possible. Read, discuss, and summarize 2 Corinthians 7:8–11. If we have "godly sorrow," we can improve, learn, and grow from our mistakes. It is different from being embarrassed or ashamed. Godly sorrow leads to true repentance, or change. When we repent, does that mean we just say the words "I'm sorry," and then everything is fine? Help them see that repentance means more than that.

Road to Repentance Activity

- Cut out the pieces from the Week 37 Activity Sheets. Read and discuss the quote on the back of the steering wheel.

- Put the picture of Heavenly Father and Jesus on one side of the room. Put the "Sin" sign on the opposite side of the room.

- Have kids stand in the middle of the room while holding the repentance steering wheel and pretend to drive an imaginary car.

- Give them specific scenarios and let them act out which direction their cars would be facing for each scenario. For example: You lied to your mom about eating your vegetables. Which direction are you facing? Have them point their cars toward the sin sign. If you feel "godly sorrow" for doing this, what will you do? Keep lying about it or change direction to repent? Have them turn their steering wheels to point their car toward Heavenly Father and Jesus. Explain that when we repent, we turn away from sin and turn toward God for forgiveness.

- What steps do we need to take now that we're pointed in the right direction? Set up the "Road to Repentance" pieces in a line that leads to the picture of Heavenly Father and Jesus. Have them drive their car a little closer to the Heavenly Father/Jesus picture as you discuss each step and share specific things they might do if they repent. (Tell Mom the truth, let her know I'm sorry, go back and eat my vegetables.)

- Repeat with other scenarios, letting each kid take turns holding the steering wheel.

Testify that as we truly repent when we make mistakes, we will feel closer to Heavenly Father and Jesus and become more like Them.

Note: You might want to discuss how true repentance doesn't always follow exactly the same steps, but this is a good way to practice ways to show that we have "godly sorrow."

EXTENSION

You could also let the kids make cars out of cardboard boxes to go along with this activity.

GRUMPY GIVING: Start the lesson by pretending to be really grumpy. Give each of them some kind of small toy or treat while mumbling and complaining about how you just wanted to keep the toys/treats for yourself.

Share this verse in 2 Corinthians 9:7, "Every man according as he purposeth in his heart, so let him give; not grudgingly, or of necessity: for God loveth a cheerful giver."

When we give things to others, does God want us to be grumpy about it? (No!) What word did Paul use to describe how we should act when we share things? (Cheerful.) Talk about why it's sometimes hard to be cheerful when giving things to other people and ways we can remember to be cheerful and loving while making sacrifices for others.

Discuss different things we might give to other people. Remind them that we don't always have to give material things. We can give our time and service to others. List specific things we might do or give to others (rake lawns, shovel driveways, help carry things, donate coats to others, etc.).

EMOTION GUESSING: Cut out the mood paper slips from the Week 38 Activity Sheet. Fold them and place them in a bowl. Have one person pick one out of the bowl without letting others see. Have them give a small treat or toy to another person while pretending to be in the mood listed on the paper they picked. Whoever can guess what mood they were showing gets to do the next one. After everyone has had a chance, discuss the difference it makes when we give cheerfully.

"Hope You Have a Happy Day" Tags

Cut out the tags from the Week 38 Activity Sheet. Attach them onto candy bars or some sort of treat to give to others. Let each person choose someone they want to give theirs to, such as a neighbor or a church leader, and remind them to do it cheerfully!

Testify that Heavenly Father and Jesus can help us find ways to give time, service, and material help to others around us. They have given us lots and are happy when we help others around us as well!

EXTENSION

Read and discuss "The Second Great Commandment" by Russell M. Nelson (*Ensign*, Nov, 2019).

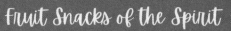
FRUIT CANDY: Get a bag of fruit snacks or another candy that includes different fruit flavors, such as Skittles. Have everyone close their eyes, take one out of the bag, and try to guess what fruit it is based on the taste. Did all of them taste exactly the same?

There are many different "flavors" of the Spirit, or ways that the Spirit speaks to us. Paul taught ways we can recognize the Spirit in our lives and what it might feel like to us. He described the ways we might feel the Spirit as "the fruit of the Spirit" (Galatians 5:22–23).

"Fruit Snacks" of the Spirit

Cut out the fruit snack bag and fruit pieces from the Week 39 Activity Sheet. Use these to teach the words Paul used in describing what the Spirit's fruits are in Galatians 5:22–23. Here are some ideas of ways you could use the pieces to teach this concept:

• Put all of the fruit pieces inside the fruit snack bag. Let everyone take turns dropping one out of the bag. As it's taken out, discuss what that word means and the times we've experienced that feeling.

• Lay all of the fruit pieces out on a table. Take turns choosing a fruit that you like. Explain why you like that fruit, discuss why that fruit of the Spirit is a good thing, and share times you've felt that feeling in your life. Put the pieces into the fruit snack bag after each is discussed.

• Hide the fruit pieces around the room. Take turns finding one and discussing each as they're found. Place them in the fruit snack bag after they're discussed.

Testify that when we feel those feelings mentioned in Galatians 5, such as love, joy, peace, etc., we are feeling the Spirit (the Holy Ghost). Remind them of how great the gift of the Holy Ghost is and how important it will be to them throughout their lives. Discuss what actions we might take in our lives that will help us walk in the Spirit daily (Galatians 5:25).

EXTENSIONS

• Read Galatians 6:7–10. Act out what it means to sow and reap. Discuss ways we can "sow" spiritual things of eternal importance in our lives rather than sowing worldly things. What blessings do we reap from the Spirit when we make these efforts?

• Discuss what the opposite words would be for each of the fruits of the Spirit.

• Memorize the names of each of the fruits of the Spirit.

• Discuss stories of things Jesus Christ did in His life that demonstrate different fruits of the Spirit. How does the Spirit help us become more like Christ?

WHAT ARE WE FIGHTING AGAINST? Explain that we might not have to fight in wars and battles during our lifetime, but we do have to fight against some really powerful things. Read Ephesians 6:10–12 and talk about what we have to fight against in our lives. Discuss some of Satan's attacks they've noticed in the world or in their own lives.

STAND! Would you expect to win a battle if you were sitting or lying down? Read Ephesians 6:11–14 out loud and have everyone stand up in a battle pose each time they hear the word "stand." What are some things we can do in our lives to stand strong in the battle against Satan?

ARMOR: Does God leave us alone in this battle? How does He help us? He might not give us metal armor, but He does give us other things to help us. Read and discuss Ephesians 6:10–18. What does God give us to help us?

Teddy Bear Armor

Get out a small teddy bear/stuffed animal/doll. Cut out the armor pieces from the Week 40 Activity Sheet. Take turns choosing a piece of armor to put on the teddy bear/stuffed animal/doll. As each is chosen, read and discuss what is on the back of that piece of armor.

If you don't have a teddy bear or doll that will work for this, you can also draw the outline of a person on a piece of paper and add the armor pieces to that picture. It would also be powerful to print actual photos of each kid to put the armor onto.

Read Ephesians 6:10 and testify that the Lord is the one who can help make us strong in this battle against Satan. Remind them of how important they are and how their faith and actions can make a big difference in this fight against Satan. Encourage everyone to choose one way to strengthen their faith and put on the armor of God in their lives.

EXTENSIONS

Find items around your house the kids can wear that can be used to represent the pieces of armor (an apron for the breastplate, belt for the girdle, stick for the sword, muffin tin or cardboard for the shield, etc.). Share ways they can actively fight against Satan through Christ's help.

For older kids, assign each kid to study and teach about the symbolism of one of the armor items in more detail.

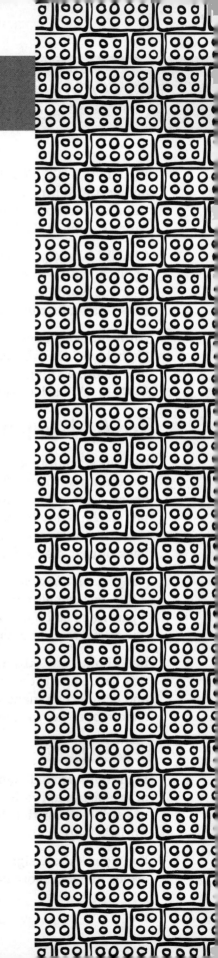

THINK OF GOOD THINGS: Philippians 4:8 teaches us that we should think about things that are true, honest, just, pure, lovely, etc. Sit in a circle and take turns listing things that fit these descriptions. See how many times you can make it around the circle without repeating anything.

Building Our Faith

Does Jesus Christ fit all of the characteristics described in Philippians 4:8? Paul taught that our faith should be "built up" in Jesus Christ (Colossians 2:7). Cut the block pieces out from the Week 41 Activity Sheet. Show the large Jesus Christ piece and remind them that He represents everything that is good. Build a large solid cube out of real blocks and tape the Jesus paper onto it. Review what we know about Jesus while building this cube. Tape the smaller paper block pieces onto real blocks. Place them in a pile and take turns choosing one from the pile. If that block describes something that would be in our lives if our faith is built upon Jesus, stack it on top of the large Christ block. If not, set it off to the side.

To simplify, skip the real blocks and glue the smaller paper blocks onto the larger paper Jesus block.

"Be Not Moved"

If our faith is built strongly in Jesus Christ, we will receive Him and walk in His ways (Colossians 2:6). Paul counsels us to "continue in the faith, grounded and settled, and be not moved away from the hope of the gospel" (Colossians 1:23). Discuss what this means and what can make this difficult to do sometimes (peer pressure, difficulty sacrificing our time to the gospel, etc.). If possible, mark off a small area using either tape or blocks. Place a picture of Jesus in the area. Let each person take turns standing inside the area while others try to get them out of it. It could be a good idea to set a rule that nobody else is allowed to go inside the circle, but they can try to tempt them to leave the circle by offering candy, a favorite game, a toy, or they could gently throw something soft, such as socks, at those in the circle.

Philippians 4:13 teaches, "I can do all things through Christ which strengtheneth me." Discuss how Christ can strengthen us as we strive to stay strong to His teachings and live like Him.

ADDITIONAL SCRIPTURES ABOUT JESUS: Paul shared many more teachings about Jesus that can help us as we strive to build our faith in Him. Read and discuss what is taught in the following verses:

Philippians 4:4	Colossians 1:14–15	Colossians 3:16–17
Philippians 4:7	Colossians 1:20	Colossians 3:23–24

Testify of the blessings we receive from building our faith and our actions upon the Gospel of Jesus Christ.

EXTENSIONS

On the back of the paper block pieces, write down specific things you will do to build your faith in Jesus (study the scriptures, pray, go to church, etc.).

Create a block tower with Jesus Christ on the bottom. Write each person's name on a block stacked on top of that to represent their willingness to keep their faith built on Jesus Christ.

Colossians 2:7 also teaches us to be "rooted" in Christ. Compare trees with shallow roots to trees with deep roots. Discuss ways we can deepen our roots in Christ to give us more spiritual strength throughout our lives.

EXTINGUISH/QUENCH: Talk about how fire extinguishers work. Find and show pictures of fires being extinguished to help them visualize this in their minds. In the scriptures, Paul counsels us to "quench not the Spirit" (1 Thessalonians 5:19). If we quench the Spirit, that means we extinguish the Holy Ghost's influence in our lives.

LIGHTING THE FIRE OF THE SPIRIT: Remind them that the Spirit brings light and knowledge into our hearts and minds. Discuss ways we can "ignite" the Spirit in our lives so that we feel its comforting, guiding, and protecting light and warmth. Explain that the flames the Spirit brings into our lives are good flames that we don't want to get rid of ("quench").

QUENCHING THE SPIRIT: Discuss this quote from David A. Bednar:

"If something we think, see, hear, or do distances us from the Holy Ghost, then we should stop thinking, seeing, hearing, or doing that thing. If that which is intended to entertain, for example, alienates us from the Holy Spirit, then certainly that type of entertainment is not for us."

Brainstorm things we might encounter that could distance us from the Spirit. Encourage everyone to pay attention to things in their lives that might "quench the Spirit" and to strive to avoid those things.

Don't Quench the Spirit Game *1 Thessalonians 5:19*

- Cut out the parts on both of the Week 42 Activity Sheets. Follow these directions to play a game to discuss ways we can ignite the Spirit and keep it glowing in our lives.

- Set out the letters from the activity sheet to spell out the word S-P-I-R-I-T.

- Take turns coloring in the different letters with an orange crayon while sharing things we can do in our lives to help us feel the warmth and light the Spirit offers us.

- Turn the letters upside down (in S-P-I-R-I-T order still). Explain that it takes work to get the Spirit burning in our lives and to keep it burning.

- The goal of this game is to "light up" (turn face up) each of the letters of "Spirit" so the whole word is glowing brightly, without any of it being "quenched" (turned face down).

- Place the cards from the activity sheet in an upside-down pile. Take turns choosing one.

- If the card shows something that would invite the Spirit into their lives, they can "light up" part of the word "Spirit" by flipping one of the letter pieces over so it is face up.

- When a letter is "quenched," you will flip that letter over to the darker back side that shows the extinguished candle.

Testify that Christ can help them feel the light of the Spirit in their lives. That light can help them get through challenges they face in life and help them in many other ways as they learn to listen to and rely on it. Explain that it's also important for them to share that light with others and to use it to fight against the darkness that Satan tries to spread on the earth. Remind them that Christ can help them relight spiritual flames when it feels like they are shrinking or have been extinguished or quenched.

EXTENSIONS

APOSTASY AND RESTORATION: 2 Thessalonians 2:1–3 mentions a "falling away" before the Second Coming of Christ. This is talking about a time called the Great Apostasy. After Christ and the Apostles died, the doctrine of Jesus Christ was corrupted and truths were lost. Demonstrate this by placing the "SPIRIT" pieces from this week's activity sheet upside down on the extinguished side. Then discuss how those truths and spiritual light were restored again through Joseph Smith. Read and discuss Joseph Smith—History 1:8–17. Flip the "SPIRIT" letters back over to the spiritual light side while discussing truths that were restored through Joseph Smith.

Sing "The Spirit of God" and discuss how the Spirit is similar to a fire.

If possible, build a real campfire with sticks. Discuss how the sticks represent our efforts to bring the Spirit into our lives. Make s'mores over the fire while discussing the sweet fruits that come into our lives through the light of the Spirit and how we're blessed by not "quenching" it.

PERILOUS TIMES: Paul explained that in the last days (the time that we're living in right now!), "perilous times shall come" (2 Timothy 3:1). He taught that many people would be "ever learning, and never able to come to the knowledge of truth" (2 Timothy 3:7). Who knows ALL things and can teach us the truths that we need to know in order to survive through these perilous times (God and Jesus)? In what ways do They teach us the truths that we need to know? Read 2 Timothy 3:14–17 and discuss what these verses say about the importance of studying scriptures. What kinds of truths can we learn from the scriptures?

HOW THE SCRIPTURES HELP TEACH US: Read 2 Timothy 3:16 once more and explain in depth what each of the phrases in it might mean. ("All scripture is given by inspiration of God, and is profitable for doctrine, for reproof, for correction, for instruction in righteousness.") If the kids you're teaching are old enough, you could have them try to memorize this verse. You could also assign each person one of the phrases from this verse to think about and explain. Share personal experiences of times we've learned important concepts from the scriptures. Remind them that if we really believe what we learn from the scriptures, it will affect the actions we take and how we live our lives.

SPIRITUAL TEACHERS: Give each person a piece of paper and something to color with. Have them draw a picture of one of their favorite stories from the scriptures. Let them take turns being "spiritual teachers" by showing their picture to everyone else and teaching them about it.

The Scriptures Make Us Wise Bookmarks

Review the phrase from 2 Timothy 3:15 which states that the scriptures "are able to make thee wise unto salvation through faith which is in Christ Jesus." Talk about what this means. How is the wisdom we learn from the scriptures more valuable than any wisdom we might gain elsewhere?

Give each person a bookmark from the Week 43 Activity Sheet. Let them color the front side of it. Encourage them to make daily scripture study a priority this week and to use the back side of their bookmark to evaluate how well they're doing with scripture study throughout the week. Depending on the age of kids, you can either have them put a checkmark by each day that they listen to scriptures, or, if they're more advanced, they could give themselves a letter grade based on how well they feel like they studied and learned from the scriptures on their own each day. It could be fun to offer some kind of small treat or prize to anyone who returns their bookmarks the next week showing that they studied from the scriptures each day.

Testify that, even if things in the world get confusing, the scriptures can help teach us the word of God, help us learn more about Christ, and help us know what is true.

Hearing and Feeling Christ's Voice

Hebrews 4:7 states, "To day if ye will hear his voice, harden not your hearts." In what ways can we hear the Lord's voice? What does it mean to harden our hearts?

Explain that the Epistle to the Hebrews contains many truths about Jesus Christ. We are going to practice LISTENING for those truths with our ears as well as trying to FEEL those truths with our hearts. Cut out the fill-in-the-blank question strips, ears, and heart from the Week 44 Activity Sheets. Tape the ears onto a headband. You can either tape the heart onto each person or make it into a necklace they can wear.

Let everyone take turns pulling out a fill-in-the-blank question strip from a pile. When they get their question strip, read the scripture on the strip out loud for them. Have them wear the ear headbands and LISTEN for the answer to the fill-in-the-blank question. After they've listened to the words and can answer the question, place the heart on them. Remind them that it's not enough just to hear the truths of the gospel of Jesus Christ. We need to also soften our hearts and FEEL what those truths about Jesus mean to us. Reread the statement on their fill-in-the-blank strip and ask what that means personally to them. Take some time to discuss each one. For example, when discussing how Hebrews 2:18 says that Christ suffered Himself to be tempted so that He can succor us when we're tempted, does that give us hope? Does it make you happy that He wants to help you?

Take turns wearing the ears/heart and answering questions.

Testify that after we hear the word of God and feel it in our hearts, it is important to act on those feelings. As we listen, feel, and act, Christ can help us become more like Him and receive blessings in our lives.

EXTENSION

Listen to some favorite songs about Jesus. Have everyone close their eyes and pay attention to how their hearts feel as they listen to the words of the songs.

WHAT IS FAITH? What does the word "faith" mean? Read and discuss Hebrews 11:1–3; 6. How can we believe in God and Jesus even when we don't see Them?

Faithful People Charades/Pictionary

When many Christians were being persecuted because of their faith in Jesus, Paul tried to encourage and inspire them by reminding them of other people who had shown incredible faith and were blessed for it.

Cut apart the name slips from the Week 45 Activity Sheet. Put them in a bowl and let everyone take turns pulling one out and either acting or drawing pictures to get the others to guess the name that was on their slip. Look up scriptures as necessary to review these stories. Discuss the incredible amount of faith shown by each of them and the blessings that came to them because of their faith.

Is it sometimes hard to stay strong in our faith? How can these examples help us?

Run the Race

Read and discuss Hebrews 12:1, that states, "Wherefore seeing we also are compassed about with so great a cloud of witnesses, let us lay aside every weight, and the sin which doth so easily beset us, and run with patience the race that is set before us."

What does it mean to "run with patience the race that is set before us?" What sins might we need to lay aside?

Cut out the race bib from the Week 45 Activity Sheet. Display the bib and discuss what it's like to run long races. What makes them difficult? Compare this to what our lifelong "race" is. What might make it difficult to keep our faith strong as we strive to become more like Christ? Discuss how Christ can help us endure whatever difficulties we face in this life as we rely on Him.

Anyone who is willing to do their best to run this "race" can sign their names on the back of the runner bib. Remind them that this is a lifelong race, and it will definitely be difficult at times, but the blessings will be great.

Read and discuss the following scriptures and discuss how Christ can help us as we "run with patience the race that is set before us."

"[Look] unto Jesus the author and finisher of our faith; who... endured the cross, despising the shame, and is set down at the right hand of the throne of God." Hebrews 12:2	"He hath said, I will never leave thee, nor forsake thee . . . The Lord is my helper, and I will not fear what man shall do unto me." Hebrews 13:5–6	"Let us draw near with a true heart in full assurance of faith." Hebrews 10:22

Testify that as we keep our focus on Christ and work to keep our faith strong despite difficulties, great things can happen, even if it takes time for us to see those great things.

JUST FOR FUN: Take turns wearing the race bib and running to a picture of Christ. Remind them that our race is a lifelong race that will take more than just a few minutes, and that the only person we're competing against is ourselves. Remind them that it's important to cheer others on in this race as well.

EXTENSIONS

Sing "True to the Faith" and discuss how we can stay true to our faith in Christ, even when it seems difficult to do.

Read "Your Four Minutes" talk by Gary E. Stevenson (*Ensign*, May 2014).

I will run with patience the race that is set before me.

121

Hebrews 12:1

TASTE TEST: Ask what the words sweet, sour, salty, and bitter mean. Then take turns blindfolding each person and giving them a small sample of food that fits each description, such as sugar or chocolate chips (sweet), lemon juice (sour), pretzels or potato chips (salty), or black pepper (bitter). Have them describe what they tasted using the words sweet, sour, salty, or bitter.

SCRIPTURES: Read James 1:26 and James 3:1–18. Talk about how the words that come out of our mouths can have a huge impact on us as well as others. James 3:11 talks about sweet vs. bitter. Does Heavenly Father want us to use our words to say sweet things or bitter things? Discuss specific sweet, kind things we can say and how those words are much better than saying mean, bitter things.

Sugar vs. Black Pepper (You will need sugar and black pepper for this activity.)

Set out a small cup. Explain that our goal is to fill this cup up with sweet sugar! Cut out the mouth pieces from the Week 46 Activity Sheet. You can either hide them around the room or put them in an upside-down pile and let everyone take turns finding/choosing one out of the pile. If what is written on that piece is a sweet thing to say, they can put a spoonful of sugar in the cup. If it is an unkind, bitter thing, they will put a spoonful of black pepper into the cup. When all of the phrases have been discussed, stir the black pepper and sugar together in the cup. Would it be hard to get all of the black pepper pieces out of the cup? Is it hard to take back mean words once they've been said?

Reread James 3:10: "Out of the same mouth proceedeth blessing and cursing . . . These things ought not so to be." Explain that we will all use words we shouldn't at some point in our life, but it's important to try to be better each day and to work to eliminate any unkind or bitter words from our lives.

Testify of the importance of using kind words. Discuss how doing so will help us become more like Christ, and remind them that Christ can help them be better at this in their lives.

JUST FOR FUN: Make and eat a treat that has lots of sugar and sweet ingredients in it, such as ice cream sundaes with many toppings or chocolate chip cookies filled with lots of types of chocolate chips/M&M's/etc. Practice giving each other kind (sweet) compliments while eating the treat.

EXTENSIONS

James 1:5–6 explains another really good way we can use words. It says, "If any of you lack wisdom, let him ask of God, that giveth to all men liberally, and upbraideth not; and it shall be given him." Have a discussion on prayer and explain that it is great to ask God when you have questions.

LIGHT: Remind them of the light that comes into our lives through Heavenly Father, Jesus Christ, and the Holy Ghost. Read and discuss 1 Peter 2:9: "But ye are a chosen generation, a royal priesthood, an holy nation, a peculiar people; that ye should shew forth the praises of him who hath called you out of darkness into his marvellous light."

Why might we be considered "a peculiar people"? What does that mean? In what ways does God bring light into our lives when we follow Him and His Son?

1 Peter 2:12 teaches that our good works can "glorify God." Share some of the good things you've noticed others do, and explain that those things can also help others feel close to God and feel His light and love for them in their lives.

Glorifying God Picture Activity

Cut out the Week 47 Activity Sheet and assemble the shape so that the picture of Heavenly Father is hidden on the inside part of it. Have everyone sit in a circle. Hand the shape to one person and let that person choose one of the categories from the outside flaps (at home, at school, with friends, etc.). Each person will take turns listing one good deed they could do in that setting as they pass the shape around the circle. Whoever is last in each round will then open up the flap for that category to demonstrate how those good deeds can help people feel God's presence in their lives. Take turns letting different people start, and, as needed, give prompts to help them think of good works they could do in each setting. (What could you do if you saw someone lonely at school? What could you do if another kid wanted a turn on the swing you were on at the park? How could you help a friend who is going through a hard time? How can being reverent at church help yourself and others feel the Spirit?) Clarify that our reason for doing good works shouldn't be to get praise for ourselves. Rather, we should do good with the intent to help others feel God's presence, light, and love in their lives.

Once all categories have been discussed, display the picture of Heavenly Father. Testify of His love for all of us. Encourage them to find ways to take actions to feel His light in their own lives, and then to help others feel His light and love in their lives as well.

EXTENSIONS

When we do good works, does that guarantee that we will never suffer, be made fun of, or go through other hard things? Read and discuss 1 Peter 4:12–16.

1 Peter 3:15 instructs us to "be ready always to give an answer to every man that asketh you a reason of the hope that is in you." Take turns role-playing to practice answering the question of where you get your hope from.

WEEK 48
1 JOHN

God and Jesus Hearts

Love Hearts

The Apostle John had personally walked and talked with Jesus Christ, so he knew firsthand about the reality of Christ, as well as the love that Jesus and Heavenly Father have for us, Their children. Give everyone a blank piece of paper. Tell them to listen carefully for the word "love" or "loveth" while you read 1 John 4:7–21. Each time they hear it, they can draw a quick heart on their paper. After reading the verses out loud, have them count how many hearts are on their paper. Does God love us a lot or a little? (A lot!) How do we know that He loves us? Reread 1 John 4:9. Discuss any other verses from this chapter that are meaningful to you.

It could also be fun to buy heart stamps to let them use for this activity.

Jesus Heart Activity

Cut out the hearts and picture of Jesus from the Week 48 Activity Sheet. There are many ways you can implement this part of the lesson. Choose one or more of the following ideas based on what you think would be the most meaningful for the kids you're teaching:

Review details about the Atonement of Jesus Christ. Take turns gluing hearts onto His picture while sharing a detail about His Atonement or a specific way that we can feel His love in our lives.

Read 1 John 2:8–11 and 1 John 4:7–8, 20–21. Discuss how if we truly love God and Jesus, we will love others around us as well. Put hearts around the Jesus picture while sharing ways we will show love to those around us.

Read 1 John 2:3–6 and 1 John 5:2–5. Discuss how we show love for God when we keep the commandments. Take turns gluing paper hearts to the Jesus picture while stating specific commandments we've been given and how obeying those shows our love for Heavenly Father and Jesus.

Read 1 John 3:1–3. Discuss how if we truly love God and Jesus, They can help us become more like Them. Glue paper hearts onto the Jesus picture while sharing Christlike characteristics that we hope to develop in ourselves.

Have everyone write their name on a heart and put those hearts around the Jesus picture. Remind them that Heavenly Father and Jesus both love us a lot. The Atonement of Jesus Christ was for the benefit of each of us individually.

John commented on how the Church in Pergamos was able to hold fast and not deny the faith (Revelation 2:13). Explain that sometimes Christians living there were put into prison and hurt for worshiping Christ. Some of them were given a chance to free themselves by cursing Christ and worshiping the emperor instead. How difficult do you think it would be to stay strong to your faith in those circumstances?

How can we similarly "hold fast" to our faith in Christ, even if it feels like we are surrounded by wickedness or feel pressure from others to deny Christ? Discuss modern-day scenarios of situations we might find ourselves in when we're tempted to let go of our faith in Christ rather than holding fast to it.

Role-Play Slips

Cut out the role-play slips from the Week 49 Activity Sheet. Take turns choosing one from a pile and role-playing how you could respond to that scenario.

BLESSINGS: Explain that Revelation 2:7 and 2:10 promise blessings to us if we're able to overcome the world. We will be able to "eat of the tree of life, which is in the midst of the paradise of God," and "if we are faithful unto death, [Christ] will give [us] a crown of life." If time allows, make paper crowns and eat some favorite fruits while talking about these blessings and how they might feel if we receive them.

Christ Wants to Help Us

Cut out the door and Jesus Christ piece from the second Week 49 Activity Sheet. Read and discuss Revelation 3:20. Have them look carefully at both sides of the door and tell you what differences they notice. Point out that the side of the door we're on has a doorknob, but the side Christ is knocking on does not. Explain that, in our lives, Jesus wants to be with us and help us, but we have to decide to open the door to let Him in. Let each person take turns holding the door in front of them while another person pretends to be Jesus knocking from the side that doesn't have a doorknob. The person holding the door will state one thing they can do to invite Christ into their lives, and then pretend to open the door.

Testify that Jesus Christ will help His followers overcome evil. He knows each of us personally, understands intimately what our challenges are, and wants to help us. Share blessings you have felt from inviting Christ into your life, trusting and following Him, and holding fast to His gospel.

Dragon and Lamb

The book of Revelation is full of many symbols. Cut out the dragon and Lamb pictures from the first Week 50 Activity Sheet. Read the scriptures on the back of them out loud while everyone tries to figure out who each animal represents (the dragon is Satan; the Lamb is Jesus Christ).

WAR: Discuss the following points made in the book of Revelation:

Revelation 13:7 explains that this dragon (Satan) is at "war with the saints" and has "power . . . over all kindreds, and tongues, and nations" (Revelation 13:7). What kind of wars does he create?

Revelation 12:17 states that Satan makes war with people who "keep the commandments of God, and have the testimony of Jesus Christ." That means that if you believe in Christ and follow Him, Satan is going to try really hard to attack you. He knows that you'll be happy if you're on the Lord's side, and Satan doesn't want us to be happy. What might his attacks look like?

Satan tries to deceive us, or to trick us, into believing the things he says instead of what Christ teaches (Revelation 13:11–14). What deceptions do we see in the world today? Are there things the world teaches that go against what God and Jesus have taught us? How can we know what to believe and who to trust?

Revelation 13:7 teaches that Satan will have power to overcome many, including the Saints of God. How can relying on Jesus Christ and listening carefully to the Spirit help us not to be overcome by this dragon?

Explain that we will go through "great tribulation" as we participate in this war with the dragon, but because of "the blood of the Lamb," we will be okay (Revelation 7:14). Explain that the "blood of the Lamb" refers to Christ and His suffering and Atonement for us.

Dodgeball War

Divide the room in half with tape or rope. Place the Lamb picture on one side and the dragon picture on the other side. Cut out the X's from the Week 50 Activity Sheet. The X's will represent injuries.

Divide everyone into two teams. Have one team go to the dragon side and one to the Lamb side. Play a game of dodgeball with soft objects, like crumpled papers or stuffed animals. Rather than having kids get "out" if they're hit, each team will tape an "X" onto their team picture if they don't catch the object when it touches them. Decide how long you will continue the game (a 5-minute time frame, playing until one team receives 10 strikes, playing until all X's have been used, etc.).

At the end of the game, have everyone sit down to talk. Point out that each team received multiple injuries. Will we receive injuries in our war against Satan? (Yes.) Discuss spiritual as well as physical injuries we might receive in this life (pain from our own sins and mistakes, hurt from the choices of others, illnesses, etc.). Do those injuries have to last forever? (No.) Read and discuss Revelation 7:14–17 and share how Revelation 12:11 says, "And they overcame him by the blood of the Lamb." Explain that Satan wants us to give up when we feel the sting from these injuries and to stop believing in Christ, but if we are faithful to Christ, eventually those pains will be taken away and replaced with joy.

Carefully remove all X's from the Lamb picture to show how Christ can heal all injuries we get from Satan. What actions do we need to take to be washed clean from our sins by the blood of the Lamb? Discuss how repentance can activate the cleansing power of the Atonement in our lives to help take away spiritual injuries. Explain that the dragon (Satan) can't and won't take away any of our injuries. Give the dragon team players the option to switch to the Lamb's side and discuss how Jesus wants to help ALL of us, but we have to choose to repent and be on His side. Regardless of how messy this war gets, Christ and His followers will win in the end. Read and discuss Revelation 15:2–4.

Testify that because of the sacrifice of the Lamb (Christ), we will be able to receive God's blessings, be washed clean from the stains we receive during this war, and eventually be able to overcome and win the war against Satan.

Babies

If possible, show baby pictures of the kids you're teaching. See if they can guess who is in each picture. If doing this with your own family, you could also include pictures of grandparents and other relatives. Talk about how special each of those babies is. Then show a picture of baby Jesus. What made His birth special? How was it the same/different from the births of other babies? Review details they know about the birth and life of Jesus.

JESUS: Remind them that Jesus is the reason we celebrate Christmas. He was born as a baby on Earth so that He could save all of us through His Atonement and Resurrection. Share testimonies of Him and what He means to us.

Nativity Wreath

Cut out the circle ornaments and wreath from the Week 51 Activity Sheets. Take turns choosing one ornament at a time. Read the scriptures on each ornament as it's chosen and discuss that part of Christ's birth story.

Listen to Christmas songs about Jesus while coloring the wreath and ornament pieces. Glue the ornament pieces onto the wreath and display somewhere as a reminder of the true reason for Christmas.

Babylon

Cut out the Babylon sign from the Week 52 Activity Sheet. Display it and ask if they've ever heard of Babylon. Explain that it represents worldliness and wickedness. Read the scriptures about Babylon on the back of the sign and ask if this sounds like a nice place to be.

"COME OUT OF" BABYLON: Explain that there are many great things in the world, but do the things that Babylon represents sound good? (No!) Babylon represents wickedness in the world. What are some things in the world we might get caught up in that could be considered wicked? Give each person time to share answers.

Revelation 18:4 teaches us to "Come out of [Babylon]." Discuss ways we can "come out of" wickedness, such as avoiding media with messages that go against the Lord's teachings, loving God more than material things, having charity, keeping the commandments, etc.

"THE HOLY CITY": If we are willing to leave Babylon, Christ invites us to inherit "the holy city, new Jerusalem" (Revelation 21:2). After Christ comes again, we will have so much joy because He will reign and be our King in a wonderful place! Use the scripture cards from the Week 52 Activity Sheet to discuss what this "holy city" will be like. Some ideas for using these cards include:

- Display the "Holy City" and Babylon signs on opposite sides of a room. Read each Holy City scripture card one at a time. Place the cards near the "Holy City" sign and discuss how it differs from Babylon. Practice running from Babylon to the "Holy City."

- Set out a gold-colored tablecloth with the "Holy City" sign on top of it. Read the cards one at a time while making models on the tablecloth of what each card describes. You could use real or edible playdough to make the models. Another option is to use frosting and candy to decorate a cake to represent the "Holy City."

- Set out a large blank piece of paper. Take turns choosing one of the scripture cards, discussing it, and drawing that aspect of the "Holy City" onto the piece of paper.

DESTRUCTION OF BABYLON: Read Revelation 18:21. Rip up the Babylon sign and throw all of the pieces in the garbage while discussing how Christ will bring an end to wickedness, sadness, and death. If we choose to follow Him, He will help us inherit much more glorious blessings than Babylon or Satan can ever offer us.

Remind them that the Second Coming will be a happy time if we choose to follow Christ and His teachings. Testify that God and Jesus love us and want to bless each of us eternally.

EXTENSIONS:

Read Jeffrey R. Holland's talk "My Words . . . Never Cease" (*Ensign*, May 2009) to deepen your discussion of Revelation 22:18–19.

An angel told her "the Lord is with thee."
Luke 1:28

She was scared when an angel came to her. The angel told her to "Fear not."
Luke 1:30

An angel told her she was going to have a son named Jesus.
Luke 1:31

She was Elisabeth's cousin.
Luke 1:36

An angel told her, "For with God nothing shall be impossible."
Luke 1:37

She told an angel, "Be it unto me according to thy word."
Luke 1:38

She said, "My spirit hath rejoiced in God my Savior."
Luke 1:47

She said, "He that is mighty hath done to me great things, and holy is his name."
Luke 1:49

He was engaged to Mary.
Matthew 1:18

An angel told him, "Fear not to take unto thee
Mary thy wife: for that which is conceived in her
is of the Holy Ghost."
Matthew 1:20

An angel told him his wife would bring forth a
son named Jesus who would save his people from
their sins.
Matthew 1:21

He "did as the angel of the Lord had bidden him."
Matthew 1:24

Frankincense

Gold

Myrrh

Cut on dotted
lines and
around outside

Fold on
solid
lines

Fold on
solid
lines

Cut on dotted
lines and
around outside

Turning Our Hearts and Minds toward Jesus Christ

John the Baptist proclaimed, "Repent ye" (Matthew 3:2). How does repentance help turn our hearts toward the Savior?

When we are baptized, our sins are washed away. How does your heart feel when you think about being completely clean?

John the Baptist taught, "He that hath two coats, let him impart to him that hath none; and he that hath meat, let him do likewise" (Luke 3:11). How can taking care of others help our hearts become more like the Savior's?

After we're baptized, we receive the gift of the Holy Ghost. How can the Holy Ghost speak to our hearts and help our hearts receive Jesus?

John the Baptist taught, "Do violence to no man, neither accuse any falsely" (Luke 3:14). How can following this counsel help us feel Christ in our hearts?

How does your heart feel when you think about Jesus?

Read John the Baptist's words in Mark 1:7 when he said, "There cometh one mightier than I after me, the latchet of whose shoes I am not worthy to stoop down and unloose." Who was he talking about?

Where was Jesus baptized (Mark 1:9)? Where were you baptized (or where will you be baptized if you aren't yet)?

Why was Jesus baptized (Matthew 3:15)? What can we do to "fulfill all righteousness" in our lives as well?

How did Heavenly Father show that He was pleased with Jesus (Luke 3:22)? Is He pleased when we are baptized as well?

Who baptized Jesus (Matthew 3:13)? Who baptized you (or who will baptize you if you aren't baptized yet)?

How was Jesus baptized (Matthew 3:16; Mark 1:9–10)? How were you baptized (or how will you be baptized if you aren't baptized yet)?

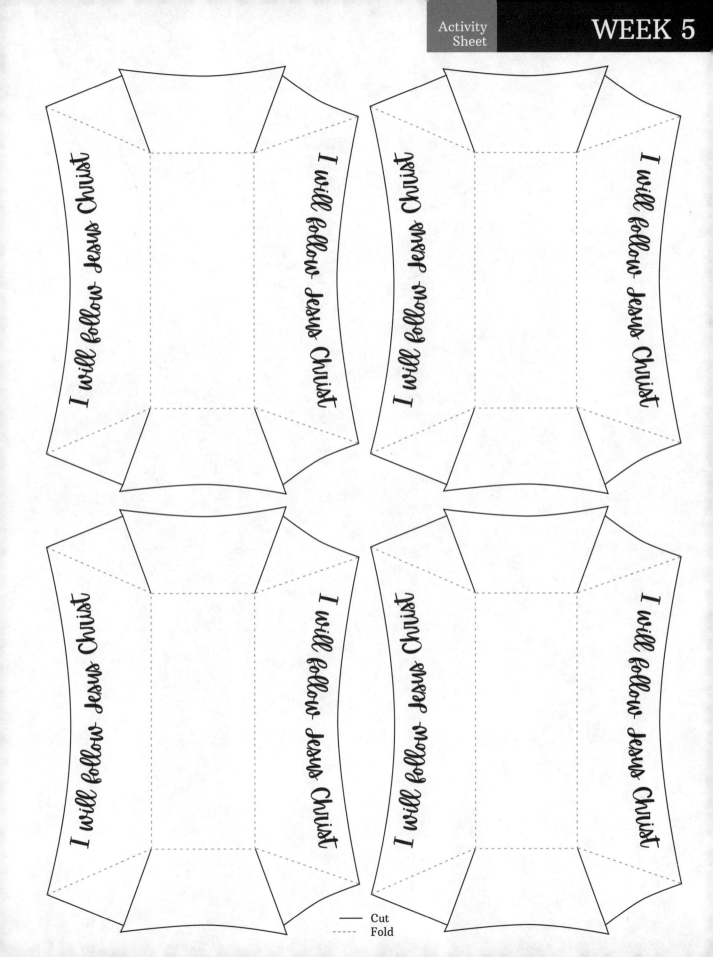

I will follow Jesus Christ

I will follow Jesus Christ

I will follow Jesus Christ

I will follow Jesus Christ

I will follow Jesus Christ

I will follow Jesus Christ

I will follow Jesus Christ

I will follow Jesus Christ

——— Cut
- - - - Fold

MUSICAL ENVELOPES

Envelope #1

Place this slip and the cup picture inside an envelope labeled #1.

Woman at The Well

Jesus Christ taught a woman of Samaria that His "living water" could bless her eternally. While she was at a well to draw water out of it, He told her that if she drank water from the well, she would be thirsty again. However, when we drink from the gospel of Christ, we will never thirst.

John 4:13–14

"Jesus answered and said unto her, Whosoever drinketh of this water shall thirst again:

But whosoever drinketh of the water that I shall give him shall never thirst; but the water that I shall give him shall be in him a well of water springing up into everlasting life."

Take turns listing things we learn from the gospel that Jesus Christ taught. As each person lists something, they can color in one of the sections of water in the picture. How do these things we learn fill our souls and keep us from thirsting spiritually?

Envelope #2

Place this slip and the baptism/spirit pieces inside an envelope labeled #2.

Being Born Again

Jesus taught a man named Nicodemus that being "born of water and of the Spirit" are important steps that lead us to living with our Heavenly Father again (John 3:5).

"Jesus answered, Verily, verily, I say unto thee, Except a man be born of water and of the Spirit, he cannot enter into the kingdom of God."

What is an ordinance we participate in that involves water (baptism)? Being baptized is like being born again of water. Take turns coloring in the water drops while explaining things we understand about baptism (In what way are we baptized? How can we prepare for baptism? How does baptism cleanse us?)

What ordinance do we participate in that involves the Spirit? Explain that after we are baptized, Heavenly Father will give us the gift of the Holy Ghost. Take turns coloring in the "Spiritual Light" pictures while explaining things we understand about the gift of the Holy Ghost. (How is it given to us? How can we feel the influence of the Holy Ghost in our lives?)

Envelope #3

Place this slip and the stone pots inside an envelope labeled #3.

Changing Water Miracle

Read John 2:1–11, which tells the story of the first miracle that was performed publicly by Jesus. Hold up a pretend glass of water each time you hear the word "water."

What did Jesus change the water into? Why?

Just like the power of Jesus Christ changed the water, His power can also change us!

Use six stone pot shapes to retell this story. Then each person will draw a picture of themselves on one of the pots. On the back side, write or draw one way the Savior can help us become more like Him and one thing we will do to invite Him into our lives.

Place in envelope #1

⌃ Place stone pots ⌃ in envelope #3

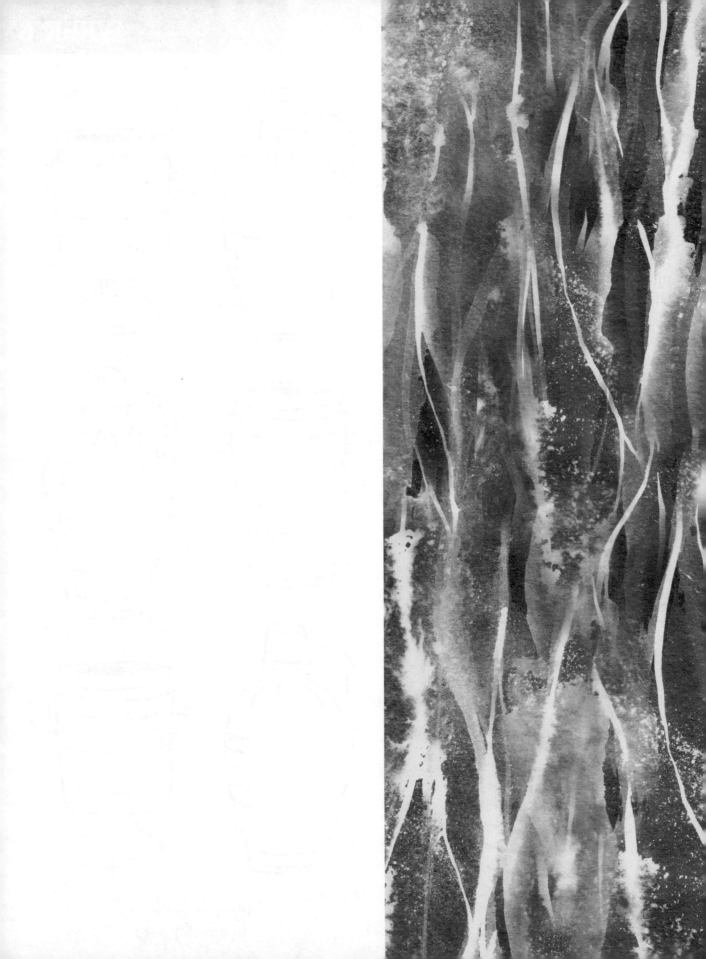

PEACE MAKER

Someone accidentally spilled paint on a picture your friend is making. Your friend is really upset. How can you be a peacemaker?

A sibling is playing with something that is yours, and you are upset that they didn't ask for your permission. How can you be a peacemaker?

Your sibling is jealous because you came home from school with a big treat and she doesn't have any treats. How can you be a peacemaker?

A parent asks you to do your chores, but you are upset because you really want to play with friends first. How can you be a peacemaker?

Two friends that you are with are arguing about what game to play. How can you be a peacemaker?

Someone spread a rumor about you at school. The teacher wants to talk to both of you about it. How can you be a peacemaker?

Another kid is making fun of your church teacher. How can you be a peacemaker?

There is only one cookie left. You really want it and feel that you've earned it, but your sibling also wants it. How can you be a peacemaker?

Someone bumped into you and you are really upset because it hurt. How can you be a peacemaker?

Your parent asks you and your siblings to clean up the living room. Two siblings are arguing about who should clean which messes in the room. How can you be a peacemaker?

Ignoring your parents and telling them you hate them	Skipping church to play video games
Going to church and participating in discussions	Saying kind words to others
Reading the scriptures and doing the things they teach	Thinking about Jesus while taking the sacrament
Being rude to others	Hurting someone
Forgiving others who have wronged you	Getting baptized and following Christ's teachings
Obeying your parents when they ask you to do something important	Saying a prayer quickly without thinking about the words
Being a peacemaker	Stealing from someone
Serving others	Saying meaningful prayers

The wise person
built his house
upon a rock.

The wise person
built his house
upon a rock.

The foolish person
built his house
upon the sand.

The foolish person
built his house
upon the sand.

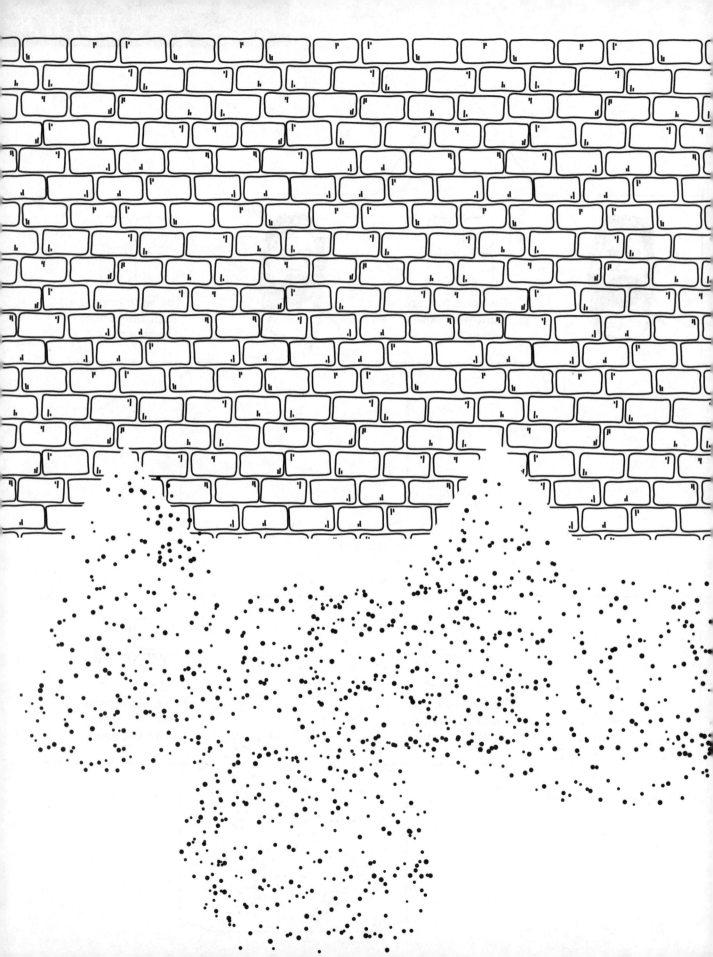

1

35 And the same day, when the even was come, he saith unto them, Let us pass over unto the other side.

36 And when they had sent away the multitude, they took him even as he was in the ship. And there were also with him other little ships.

37 And there arose a great storm of wind, and the waves beat into the ship, so that it was now full.

Mark 4:35–37

2

38 And [Jesus] was in the hinder part of the ship, asleep on a pillow; and they awake him, and say unto him, Master, carest thou not that we perish?

Mark 4:38

3

39 And he arose, and rebuked the wind, and said unto the sea, Peace, be still. And the wind ceased, and there was a great calm.

Mark 4:39

4

40 And he said unto them, Why are ye so fearful? how is it that ye have no faith?

41 And they feared exceedingly, and said one to another, what manner of man is this, that even the wind and the sea obey him?

Mark 4:40–41

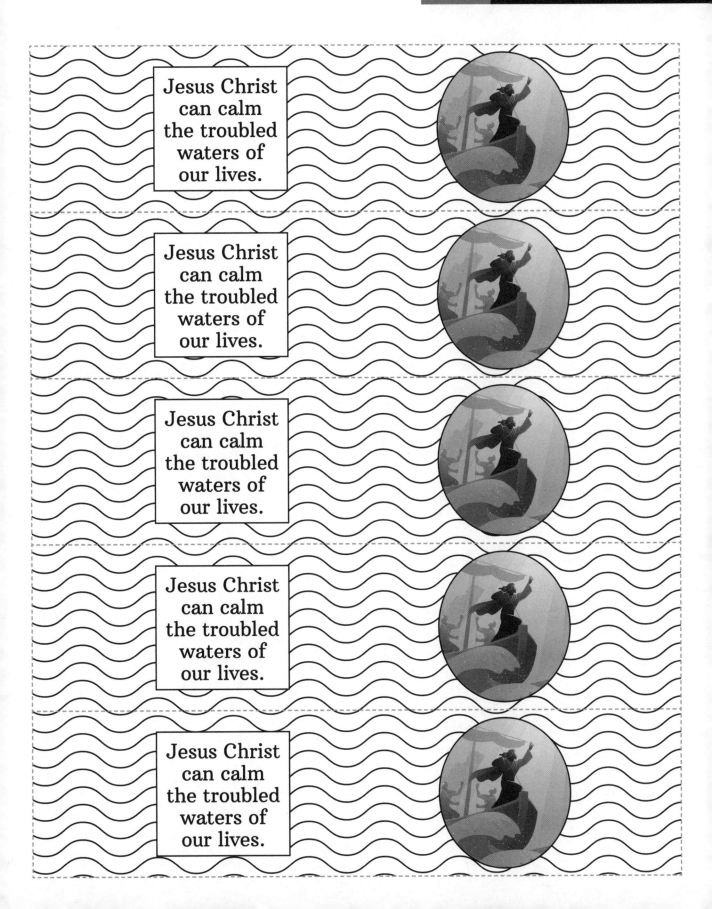

Jesus Christ can calm the troubled waters of our lives.

Jesus Christ can calm the troubled waters of our lives.

Jesus Christ can calm the troubled waters of our lives.

Jesus Christ can calm the troubled waters of our lives.

Jesus Christ can calm the troubled waters of our lives.

Jesus Christ

Me!

Simon (Peter)

Andrew

James

John

Philip

Bartholomew

Matthew

Thomas

James the Younger

Simon

Judas (Lebbaeus, Thaddaeus, Brother of James)

Judas Iscariot

Prayer Cards

Dear Heavenly Father,

When we begin our prayers, we address Heavenly Father by speaking His name reverently. How else can we show reverence while we pray?

Dear Heavenly Father,

Read the Lord's prayer in Matthew 6:9–13 and Luke 11:1–4. How did He address His Father? What are some things He prayed for?

I Thank Thee . . .

Set a timer for one minute and list as many people as you can think of who you are grateful for in your life. Remember to thank Heavenly Father for these people in your prayers!

I Thank Thee . . .

Everyone share quick summaries of the best things that have happened to them in their lives. Remember to thank Heavenly Father for these things in your prayers!

I Thank Thee . . .

What are some things we have learned from the gospel of Jesus Christ that we are thankful for? Try to think of at least ten things. Remember to thank Heavenly Father for these things in your prayers!

I Thank Thee . . .

Take a quick walk around the area you're in right now. Look for as many things as you can find that you can thank Heavenly Father for when you pray.

I Ask Thee . . .

Take turns acting out times when you might be scared, worried, or nervous. How can Heavenly Father help us when we pray for help during these times?

I Ask Thee . . .

True or False: Heavenly Father and Jesus will get mad if you ask them for forgiveness when you pray.

In the Name of Jesus Christ, Amen.

True or False: When we pray in Christ's name, we will be given ANYTHING we want, even if it's something Heavenly Father and Jesus know is not good for us.

Tares look a lot like wheat. Wheat is good. Tares are harmful weeds. Do we want to be like tares or wheat? How can we stay good like wheat even when there are bad things around us?

The Parable of
The
Wheat AND THE **Tares**

The kingdom of heaven is like a mustard seed. How big is a mustard seed? Could it grow to be very big? How can the kingdom of heaven grow? How can we help it grow?

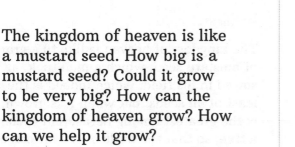

The Parable of
The
Mustard Seed

The kingdom of heaven is like leaven. Leaven is something put in bread dough to make it rise. A little bit of it can make a big change. What little things can we do to make big changes on Earth?

The Parable of
The
Leaven

The kingdom of heaven is like hidden treasure and a pearl of great price. The things Jesus teaches are worth more than anything else in the world. What things can we give up to show God that we love His gospel above all else?

The Parable of
The
**The Hidden Treasure &
The Pearl of Great Price**

wheat   tares

Read Matthew 13:24-30, 36-43

This parable teaches of tares growing together with wheat. Similarly, wickedness and righteousness are both growing together in our days. They will continue to grow together until the end of the world.

Matthew 13:31–32

The kingdom of heaven is like to a grain of mustard seed, which a man took, and sowed in his field: which indeed is the least of all seeds: but when it is grown, it is the greatest among herbs, and becometh a tree, so that the birds of the air come and lodge in the branches thereof.

Matthew 13:33

The kingdom of heaven is like unto leaven, which a woman took, and hid in three measures of meal, till the whole was leavened.

Matthew 13:44–46

The kingdom of heaven is like unto a treasure hid in a field; the which when a man hath found, he hideth, and for joy thereof goeth and selleth all that he hath, and buyeth that field. Again, the kingdom of heaven is like unto a merchant man, seeking goodly pearls: Who, when he had found one pearl of great price, went and sold all that he had, and bought it.

The kingdom of heaven is like a net. Not all fish caught in nets are good. The bad fish are cast away. Heavenly Father will one day separate the good people from the bad people. How can we live good lives?

The Parable of
The
Net

Matthew 13:52

The gospel is full of treasures (things that are of great worth). Some treasures are old. Some are new. What are some treasures that were given to us a long time ago? (Bible, etc.) What are some treasures that are newer? Can both old and new treasures be important?

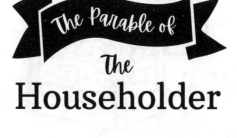

The Parable of
The
Householder

The word of God is like a seed. Not all seeds grow well. What can we do to help seeds grow big? What can we do to help our testimonies grow to be big and strong?

The Parable of
The
Sower

Cut and glue petals to center circle.

I Can Do Many Things to Help My Testimony Grow

Matthew 13:47–50

The kingdom of heaven is like unto a net, that was cast into the sea, and gathered of every kind: Which, when it was full, they drew to shore, and sat down, and gathered the good into vessels, but cast the bad away. So shall it be at the end of the world: the angels shall come forth, and sever the wicked from among the just, and shall cast them into the furnace of fire: there shall be wailing and gnashing of teeth.

Matthew 13:52

Every scribe which is instructed unto the kingdom of heaven is like unto a man that is an householder, which bringeth forth out of his treasure things new and old.

Read Matthew 13:3 23; Luke 8:4-15

If I want the word of God to grow in my heart, I need to prepare my heart to receive it.

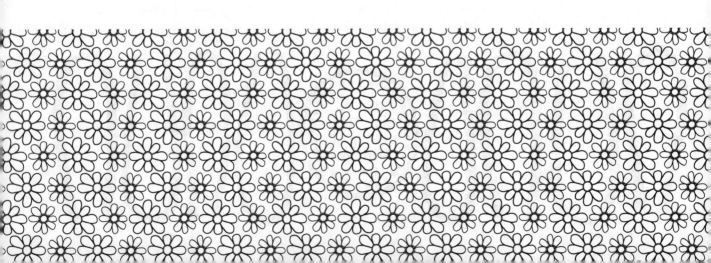

Cut on the dotted lines. Fold the corners in and tape into a basket shape. Tape the strip across the top for the handle.

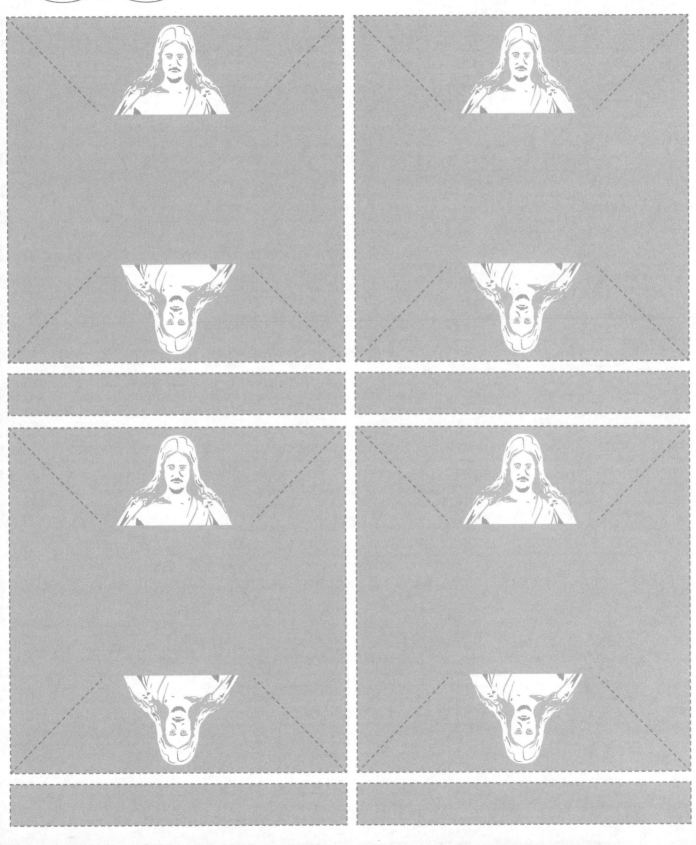

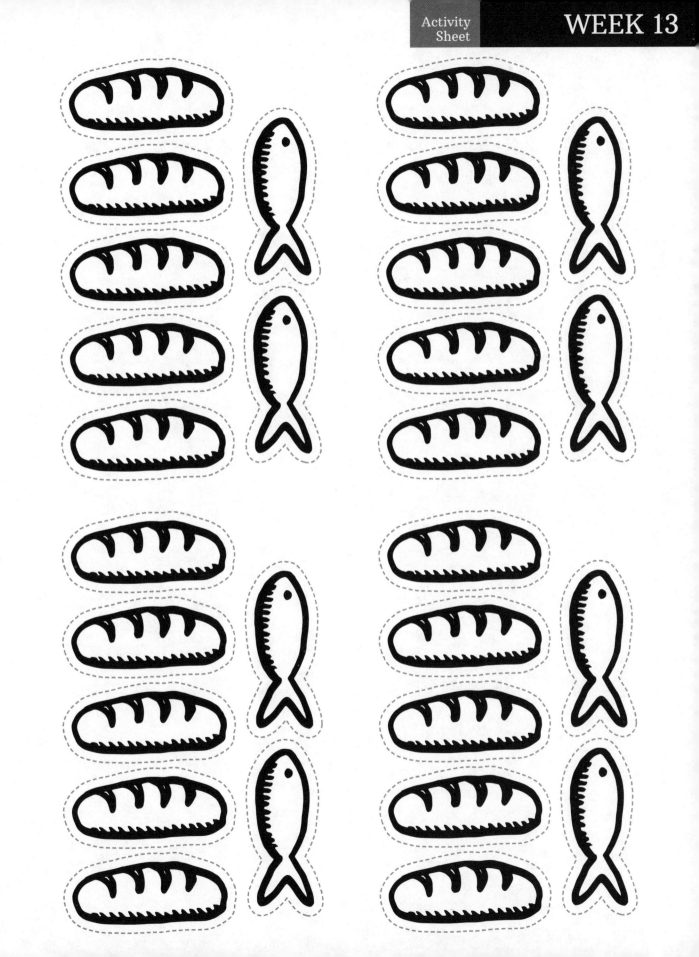

Christ Is Risen Rolls

Ingredients: large marshmallows, melted butter, cinnamon and sugar mixture, biscuit dough

1

Because Heavenly Father loves us, He sent Jesus Christ to the earth to save us (John 3:16–17).

Each person will get a white marshmallow to represent Jesus, who was sinless.

2

Jesus Christ showed how much He loves us when He suffered and died for us so that our sins can be forgiven.

Dip the marshmallow in melted butter and roll it in the cinnamon and sugar mixture to represent Christ being willing to take our sins upon Himself (Mark 14:32–42).

3

After Jesus died, He was wrapped in linen (Mark 15:46).

Flatten out a piece of biscuit dough to represent the linens Jesus was wrapped in. Wrap the biscuit around the marshmallow and pinch the edges to seal it. Make sure to seal the edges tightly!

4

Jesus's body was put in a tomb and His spirit went to heaven.

Cover the ball of dough with melted butter. Then roll the dough in the cinnamon and sugar mixture. Place seam-side down in a muffin tin.

5

The body of Jesus was in the tomb for 3 days (Matthew 12:40).

Put the rolls in the oven and bake at 375 degrees Fahrenheit for 12–15 minutes. Give them some time to cool.

6

On the Sunday morning after Jesus died, women visited Jesus's tomb and found it empty. Angels told them, "He is not here, for He is risen." (Matthew 28:1–10).

Break open the roll and look inside. It is empty, just like the tomb on Easter morning! Jesus was resurrected. He lives. He loves us. Because of this, all of us will live again after we die.

Images for this activity created by and used with permission from Crystal Wallace (www.theredcrystal.org).

1. Because Heavenly Father loves us, He sent Jesus Christ to the earth to save us (John 3:16–17).

Jesus Christ showed how much He loves us when He entered and died for us so that our sins can be forgiven.

A Firefighter

A Doctor

A Friend

A Teacher

A Kind Neighbor

A Dentist

A Parent

An Ambulance Driver

Jesus

"Thou art the Christ, the Son of the living God"
Matthew 16:16

Good Samaritan Story Figures:

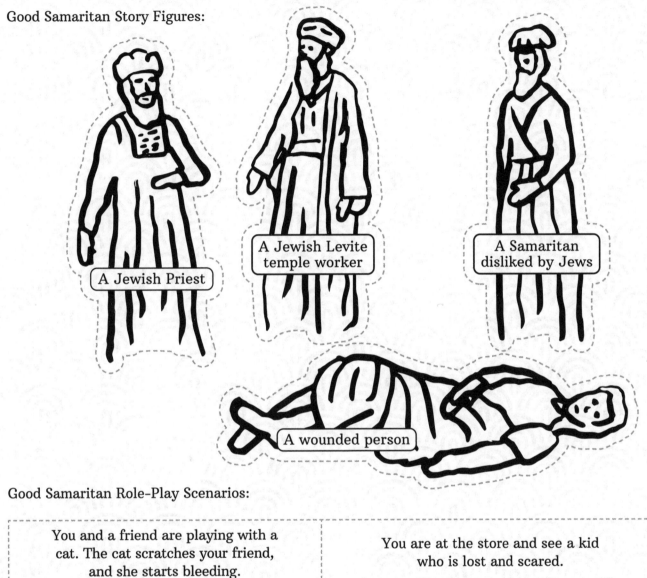

A Jewish Priest

A Jewish Levite temple worker

A Samaritan disliked by Jews

A wounded person

Good Samaritan Role-Play Scenarios:

You and a friend are playing with a cat. The cat scratches your friend, and she starts bleeding.	You are at the store and see a kid who is lost and scared.
A neighbor has been really sick and can't leave their house.	A kid at school doesn't have any food to eat at lunch and looks hungry.
Someone at school is crying. You don't know their name, but they look really sad.	Your church teacher is having a hard time because a kid in the class keeps being disruptive.
A student in your class is frustrated because they can't figure out how to swing on the monkey bars during recess. You're really good at the monkey bars, but playing in the field with your best friends sounds more fun than helping this other student learn.	A girl at school made fun of you and said unkind things to you. The next day, she slipped and spilled her lunch. Lots of other kids are laughing at her.
A lady in your neighborhood lives by herself and has told you she loves visitors.	A kid at school doesn't seem to have any friends.

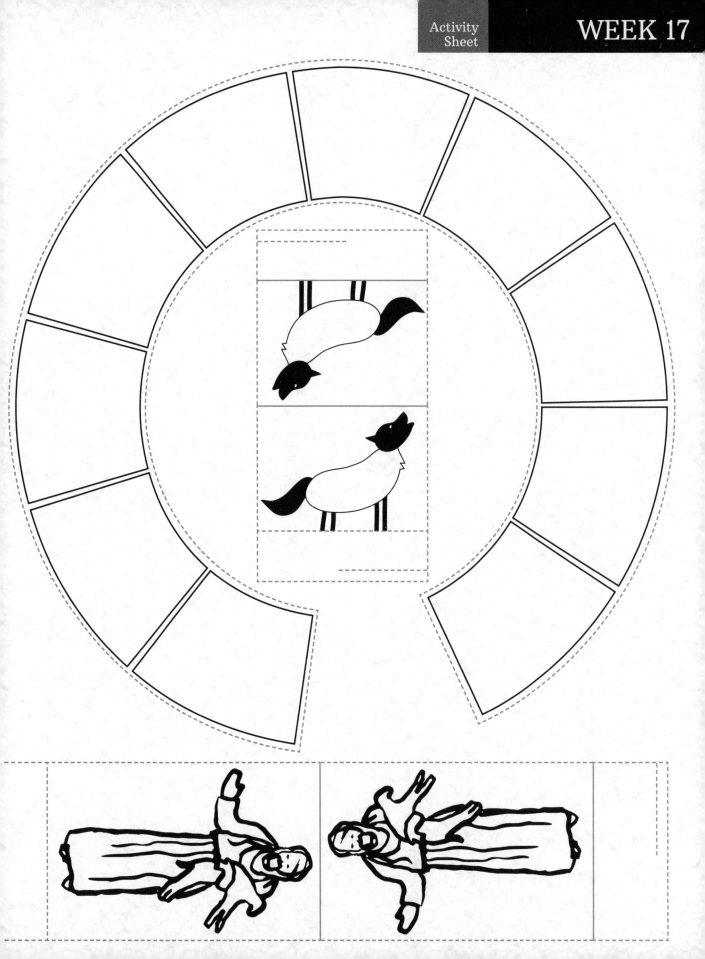

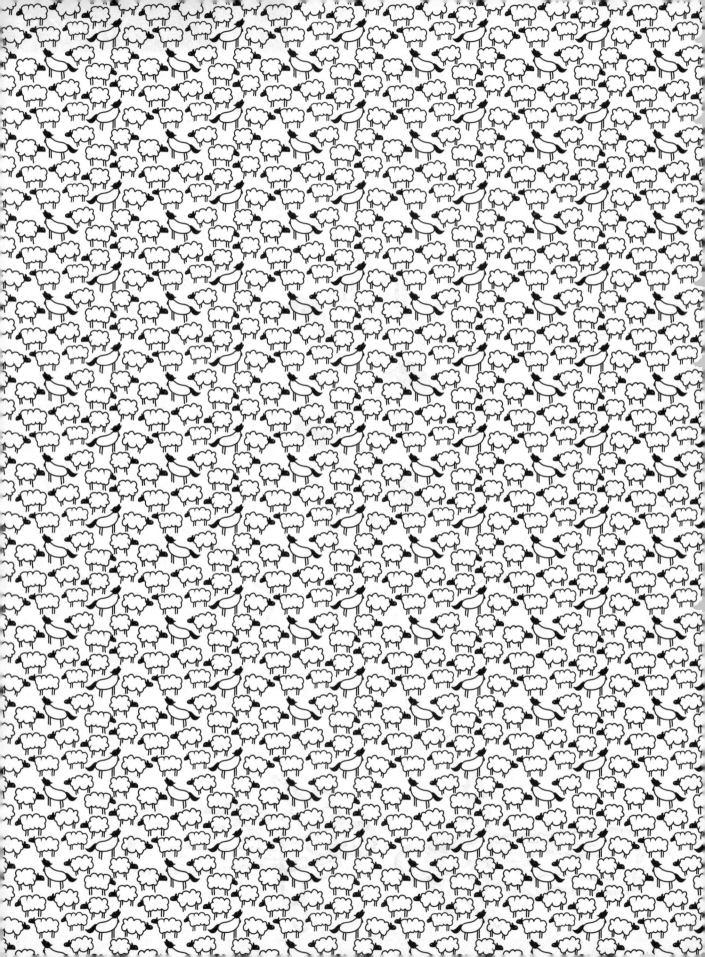

How can you hear Christ's voice when you're reading the scriptures?

How can you hear Christ's voice when you're at church?

How can you hear Christ's voice when you're listening to Church leaders?

What might Christ's voice sound like when He's asking you to serve others?

Name two commandments Christ has given us.

How does your heart feel when you're following Christ?

True or False: One thing Christ has asked us to do is to be baptized.

What might Christ's voice sound like if He's asking you to repent?

True or False: Jesus Christ knows my name and loves me.

If Christ spoke to you right now, what do you think His voice would sound like?

True or False: One thing Christ has asked us to do is to be unkind to others.

True or False: Listening to and following Christ's voice will lead you to eternal misery.

TAILS! QUESTION COINS

Cut apart and place upside down in a pile. Take turns flipping a real coin. Whenever the tossed coin lands on the tail side, whoever tossed it will pick a coin from the question pile to read and discuss.

Isaiah 53:6 states, "All we like sheep have gone astray; we have turned every one to his own way." Explain what this means to you.

What things might we do that help us feel closer to God? What things might we do that make us feel distanced from Him?

What types of songs help you feel closer to God? Choose a favorite song about Heavenly Father or Jesus to sing with everyone.

Role-play how you might respond when your friends try to get you to do something that you know will distance your heart and mind from Jesus.

True or False: The Atonement and Christ's teachings can help us find our way back to Him when we are lost.

How did the people in the parables in John 15 feel when they found what was lost?

Name three things you can do to keep Christ close to your heart this week.

Read Luke 15:20–24. List three things the father did for his son when he returned.

True or False:

God loves me a lot!

HEADS! COIN NECKLACES

Cut a hole at the top and string yarn or ribbon through it to make a necklace. Take turns flipping a coin. Whenever the tossed coin lands on the head side, the person who tossed it will give a necklace to the person sitting closest to them. Let each person write their own name on the blank line.

The Candy Sacrifice Game!

A friend outside is cold. Place two candies on the heart if you're willing to let them borrow your gloves.

FUN SPOT!
Tell a funny joke that you know!

Someone upset you. If you choose to forgive them, place one of your candies on the heart in the middle of the board to represent your sacrifice.

Your parents ask you to stop playing so you can help a neighbor. Place three candies on the heart in the middle of the board if you choose to make this sacrifice.

A song you're listening to has an unkind message. Place one candy on the heart if you decide to change the song, even though you thought it sounded like a really fun song.

Directions:

- Each person will choose one candy game piece to represent themselves. Place it on any blank space on the game board.

- Give everyone a baggie with the same amount of small treats in it, such as 15 Skittles or M&M's.

- Take turns rolling a die and moving your game piece clockwise around the board.

- If you land on a sacrifice square, you can choose to make the sacrifice or not.

- Decide beforehand how long you want to play this game. Some options could be to set a timer for 5 minutes, let everyone take 5 turns, or to continue until one person completely runs out of their candies.

- Whoever has the least amount of candies left at the end of the game is the winner, since that means they made the most sacrifices!

- Jesus promised the young man that he would receive "treasure in heaven" if he made the sacrifices asked of him (Matthew 19:21). Discuss ways we are blessed when we make sacrifices.

It's Sunday! If you choose to go to church, place two of your candies on the heart in the middle of the board to represent the sacrifice of time you've given to the Lord.

Count how many candies you have right now. If you choose to follow the commandment to pay tithing, place 10% of your treats on the heart in the middle of the board.

FUN SPOT!
Give everyone a sincere compliment!

You're in line to buy ice cream. Someone behind you asks if they can go before you because they're in a hurry. Place one candy on the heart if you're willing to make this sacrifice.

There are 2 cookies left, 1 big and 1 small. Your sister really wants the big one. Place two candies on the heart in the middle of the board if you choose to sacrifice and let your sister have the big cookie.

Candy Game Pieces:

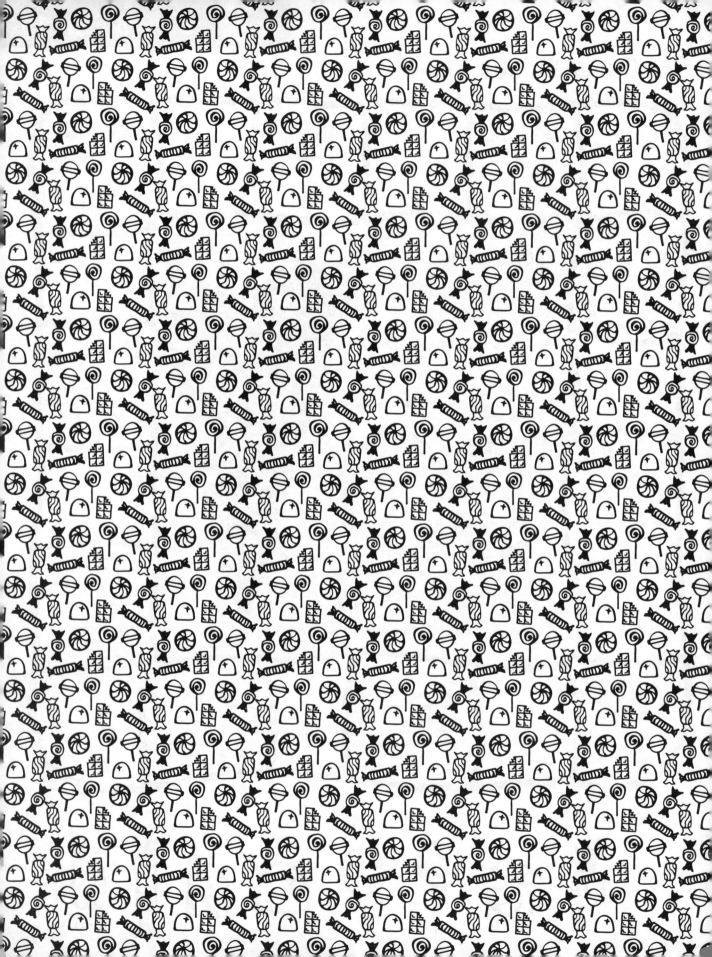

I Can Show **LOVE** to God and Others

Taking flowers to someone who's sad

Making fun of others because they're different than you are

Telling others you don't believe in Christ because you're worried they'll make fun of you

Sharing your testimony with someone in a loving way

Helping a neighbor carry grocery bags into their house

Sending a care package to someone in need

Inviting others to come to church with you

Doing something you know you shouldn't do because your friends dare you to

Walking past someone who is hurt

Helping someone who is hurt

Playing with someone who is lonely

Following God's commandments

Answering a friend's questions about a picture of Christ hanging up in your home

Telling someone you're better than them

I Can Prepare for the
Second Coming
of Jesus Christ

Preparation Sorting Cards:

Praying for guidance from the Holy Ghost	Reading and studying scriptures	Going to church	Paying tithing
Repenting of sins	Getting baptized	Going to the temple	Keeping the commandments
Making fun of Church leaders	Being irreverent during family scripture study	Lying about mistakes	Breaking the commandments

1 THE SAVIOR'S LAST SUPPER WITH HIS DISCIPLES

Jesus broke and blessed sacramental bread at the Last Supper.

Read Matthew 26:26–30. Jesus said, "This do in remembrance of me" (Luke 22:19).

How can we better remember Christ and what He willingly went through each time we partake of the sacrament?

2 THE SAVIOR WASHED THE FEET OF HIS DISCIPLES

John 13:1–17

"In the midst of [the Last Supper], Christ quietly arose, girded himself as a slave or servant would, and knelt to wash the Apostles' feet. (See John 13:3–17.) This small circle of believers in this scarcely founded kingdom were about to pass through their severest trial, so he would set aside his own increasing anguish in order that he might yet once more serve and strengthen them. It does not matter that no one washed his feet. In transcendent humility he would continue to teach and to cleanse them. He would to the final hour—and beyond—be their sustaining servant. As John wrote, who was there and watched the wonder of it all, 'Having loved his own which were in the world, he loved them unto the end' (John 13:1).

"So it had been, and so it was to be—through the night, and through the pain, and forever. He would *always* be their strength, and no anguish in his own soul would ever keep him from that sustaining role" (Elder Jeffrey R. Holland, "He Loved Them unto the End," *Ensign*, Nov. 1989).

3 OUR SAVIOR SUFFERED IN THE GARDEN OF GETHSEMANE

Jesus Christ submitted His will to His Heavenly Father and went through a lot of pain in His body and soul in Gethsemane.

Read Matthew 26:36–46.

"There in the garden bearing the Hebrew name of Gethsemane—meaning 'oil-press'—olives had been beaten and pressed to provide oil and food. There at Gethsemane, the Lord 'suffered the pain of all men, that all . . . might repent and come unto him.' He took upon Himself the weight of the sins of all mankind, bearing its massive load that caused Him to bleed from every pore" (President Russell M. Nelson, "The Atonement," *Ensign*, Nov. 1996).

4 OUR SAVIOR WAS BETRAYED, ARRESTED, AND PUT ON TRIAL

Read Matthew 26:1–5, Matthew 26:14–16, Matthew 26:21–25, and Matthew 26:47–68.

"Imagine the Being whose power, whose light, whose glory holds the universe in order, the Being who speaks and solar systems, galaxies, and stars come into existence—standing before wicked men and being judged by them as being of no worth or value!

"When we think of what he could have done to these men who took him to judgment, we have a new and different sense of his condescension. When Judas led the soldiers and the high priests to the Garden of Gethsemane and betrayed him with a kiss, Jesus could have spoken a single word and leveled the entire city of Jerusalem. When the servant of the high priest stepped forward and slapped his face, Jesus could have lifted a finger and sent that man back to his original elements. When another man stepped forward and spit in his face, Jesus had only to blink and our entire solar system could have been annihilated. But he stood there, he endured, he suffered, he condescended" (Gerald N. Lund, *Latter-day Commentary on the Book of Mormon*, compiled by K. Douglas Bassett, 37).

BOOKMARKS

Color pictures of each station in the different sections. Then write your testimony
of Jesus Christ on the back.

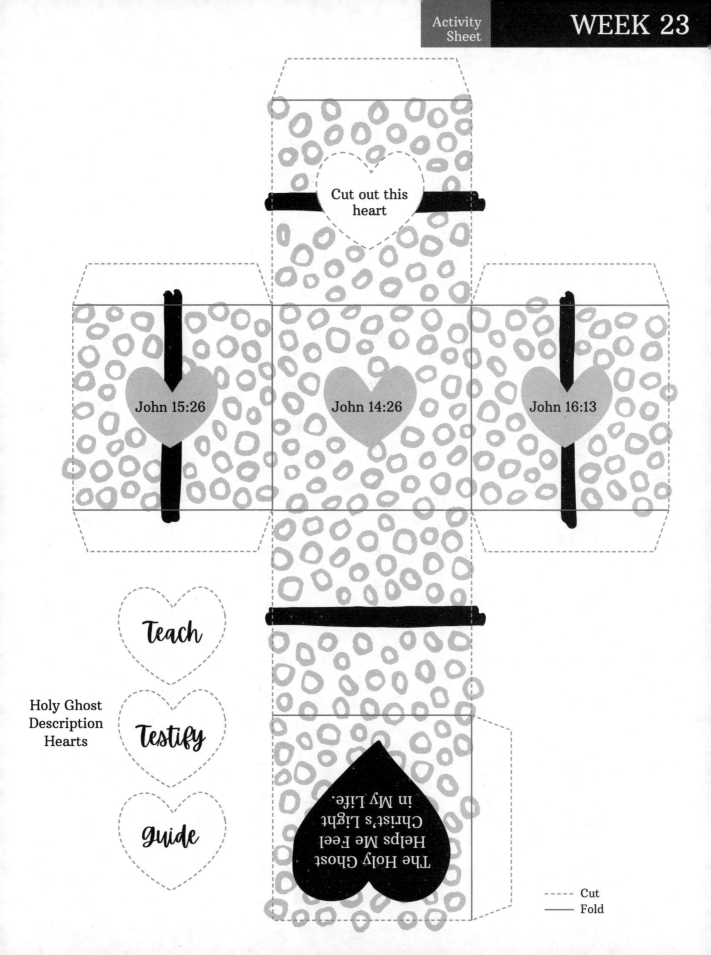

Cut out this
heart

John 15:26

John 14:26

John 16:13

Teach

Holy Ghost
Description
Hearts

Testify

Guide

The Holy Ghost
Helps Me Feel
Christ's Light
in My Life.

- - - Cut
——— Fold

"And there appeared an angel unto him from heaven, strengthening him."

Luke 22:43

"And there appeared an angel unto him from heaven, strengthening him."

Luke 22:43

"And there appeared an angel unto him from heaven, strengthening him."

Luke 22:43

"And there appeared an angel unto him from heaven, strengthening him."

Luke 22:43

"And there appeared an angel unto him from heaven, strengthening him."

Luke 22:43

"And there appeared an angel unto him from heaven, strengthening him."

Luke 22:43

"And there appeared an angel unto him from heaven, strengthening him."

Luke 22:43

"And there appeared an angel unto him from heaven, strengthening him."

Luke 22:43

1 Crown of Thorns and Purple Robe Mark 15:17–20

2 Cross John 19:15–19; Mark 15:20–21

3 Soldiers Casting Lots John 19:23–24

4 Sponge with Vinegar Mark 15:34–37

5 Earthquake and Veil of Temple Rent Matthew 27: 51; 54

6 Tomb John 19:38–42

1 Crown of Thorns and Purple Robe Mark 15:17–20

2 Cross John 19:15–19; Mark 15:20–21

3 Soldiers Casting Lots John 19:23–24

4 Sponge with Vinegar Mark 15:34–37

5 Earthquake and Veil of Temple Rent Matthew 27: 51; 54

6 Tomb John 19:38–42

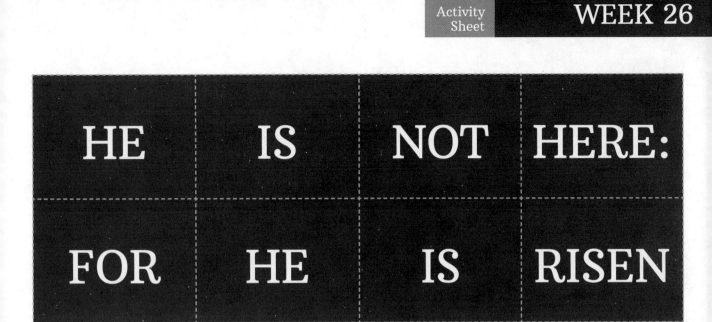

| HE | IS | NOT | HERE: |
| FOR | HE | IS | RISEN |

Place the body in the tomb without the spirit while discussing how our bodies and spirits are separated at death. Place the spirit piece behind the body while discussing the Resurrection of Jesus Christ. Discuss how we will all be resurrected after death because of Christ's victory over death. Our bodies and spirits will never again be divided.

Christ's Spirit

Christ's Body

⌐ Attach round stone to the tomb with a brad. Connect where the circles are.

Honest Oscar

Dishonest Darius

Possible Situations:

You took something from a sibling and your parents ask who took it.	Your mom asks you not to go to a certain place, but you really want to go there.
You broke your friend's toy and feel embarrassed about it.	You're at a store with a friend and the friend says you should steal a piece of candy with her.
You find some money at school that is not yours.	Your school friend hurt another kid and the teacher is asking you about what happened. You don't want to get your friend in trouble but you saw what happened.
You forgot to do your homework and your teacher is asking you if it's done.	A neighbor said they'd pay you $10 for doing some yard work for them, but they accidentally gave you two ten-dollar bills.

Sorting Cards:

You get a bad feeling about going somewhere a friend asks you to go. You ignore the bad feeling and go there anyway.	Others make fun of you for believing in Christ. You continue to learn about Him and pray to strengthen your faith in Him anyway.	A song starts playing that has words that make you feel uncomfortable. You ask if the song can be changed.	Your brother's favorite bouncy ball falls through the sewer grate, and he is very sad to have lost it. You decide to give him some of your own money to buy a new one.	Some students at school are looking at inappropriate pictures. You walk away and let an adult know, even though it might make the other kids upset with you.
You made a mistake. You feel really bad about it, so you repent and try not to make the same mistake again.	You make a mistake and decide to lie about it so you won't get in trouble.	Your family is studying the scriptures, but you decide to play with toys instead of participating.	You try to read the scriptures on your own, even though some of the words seem hard to understand.	You decide to follow the example of Jesus Christ and get baptized.
You're mad at a friend so you tell them they can't have a turn in the game you're playing.	You think about Jesus while you are taking the sacrament.	You share your testimony about Jesus Christ.	You help someone who is sad.	You make fun of someone who is teaching about Jesus Christ and His gospel.

CHRIS TIAN

Possible Scenarios:

You go to church and then forget about Jesus until the next Sunday when you go to church again.	You say mean things about another person.
You do something to help somebody.	You see your neighbor bringing in groceries and offer to help them carry their bags.
You listen to someone who's going through a hard time and treat them with love.	Your friend scrapes her knee while you're playing outside with her. You help her clean it off and put a Band-Aid on it.
You tell someone at school you're better than them because you go to church and they don't.	You yell at your sibling.
You kindly invite an interested friend to come to church with you.	You help Mom/Dad wipe off the table.
You listen reverently to the speakers and your teacher at church.	You surprise another family member by making their bed for them.
You fold your arms, close your eyes, and reverently listen to the words of a prayer.	You go to church but say mean things to a kid in your church class.
You tell someone how happy Christ helps you feel.	You are kind to all of Heavenly Father's children, even those who are different from you.

CHRISTIAN

NOT CHRISTLIKE

God made
the world
and all
things
therein

Acts 17:24

God giveth
to all life,
and breath,
and all
things

Acts 17:25

In God we
live, and
move, and
have our
being

Acts 17:28

Jesus Christ
suffered and
rose again
from the
dead

Acts 17:3

Jesus is the
Christ

Acts 17:3

If we seek
the Lord, we
will find Him

Acts 17:27

God is not
far from us

Acts 17:27

The Godhead
is not made
out of gold,
silver, or
stone

Acts 17:29

We are the
offspring of
God

Acts 17:29

Paul

HEAVENLY FATHER
and
JESUS
are with us during
hard times

Cut out the curtains. Attach them to a shoebox, cereal box, or cracker box. Add cardboard to the back of the curtain paper for extra sturdiness. Cut a hole in the top of the box to slide the puppets through.

GOD

I am not ashamed of the Gospel of Christ. Romans 1:16

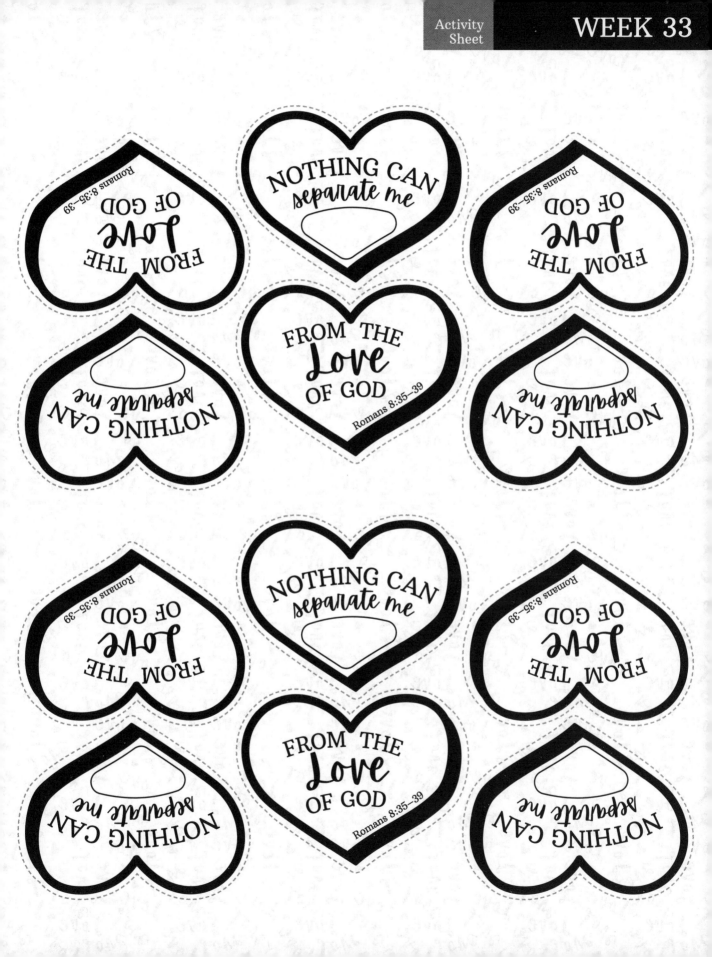

Fruits

Vegetables

A good amount of rest

Too much or too little sleep

Exercise

Cigarettes

Vaping

Alcohol

Good hygiene

Water

Drugs that have not been prescribed by a doctor

Tobacco products

Coffee or tea

Too many sweets

Grains

- - - - Cut
——— Fold

Your body is the temple of the Holy Ghost which is in you.

1 CORINTHIANS 6:19

Charity
suffereth long

Charity
doth not behave
itself unseemly

Charity
rejoiceth not in
inquity, but rejoiceth
in the truth

Charity
is kind

Charity
seeketh not her own

Charity
beareth all things

Charity
envieth not

Charity
is not easily provoked

Charity
believeth all things

Charity
vaunteth not itself

Charity
thinketh no evil

Charity
hopeth all things

Charity
is not puffed up

Charity
endureth all things

Role-play how you could show charity when kids at school try to spread mean rumors about another student.

Role-play how you could show charity if you're on a long road trip and the sibling you're sitting next to keeps interrupting you while you're trying to read a book.

Role-play how you could show charity while having dinner with a friend's family (use your manners, offer to help clean, etc.).

Role-play how you could show charity if you see a neighbor crying on the sidewalk outside.

Role-play how you could show charity if there's a kid in your class who others are making fun of.

Role-play how you could show charity if you're at home and there's only one cookie left but you know others want it too.

Role-play one way you could show love to God and Jesus by learning about Them.

Role-play how you could show charity if a sibling received a toy for their birthday that you have been wanting for a long time.

Role-play how you could show charity if a sibling keeps poking you with their finger.

Role-play how you could show charity if a friend's family member passes away and they ask you where you think their family member is now.

Role-play how you could show charity by secretly doing a good deed without letting others notice.

Role-play how you could show charity if someone who has been rude to you trips and falls.

Role-play how you could show charity to others, even when you've had a long and tiring day.

Role-play how you could show charity if you won a contest that your best friend was hoping to win.

Cut and glue sun rays to center circle.

"_____ is swallowed up in victory"

1 CORINTHIANS 15:54

"If _____ be not raised, your faith is vain"

1 CORINTHIANS 15:17

Christ

alive

sting

"In Christ shall all be made _____"

1 CORINTHIANS 15:22

Death

Jesus Christ takes away "_____ the of death"

1 CORINTHIANS 15:56

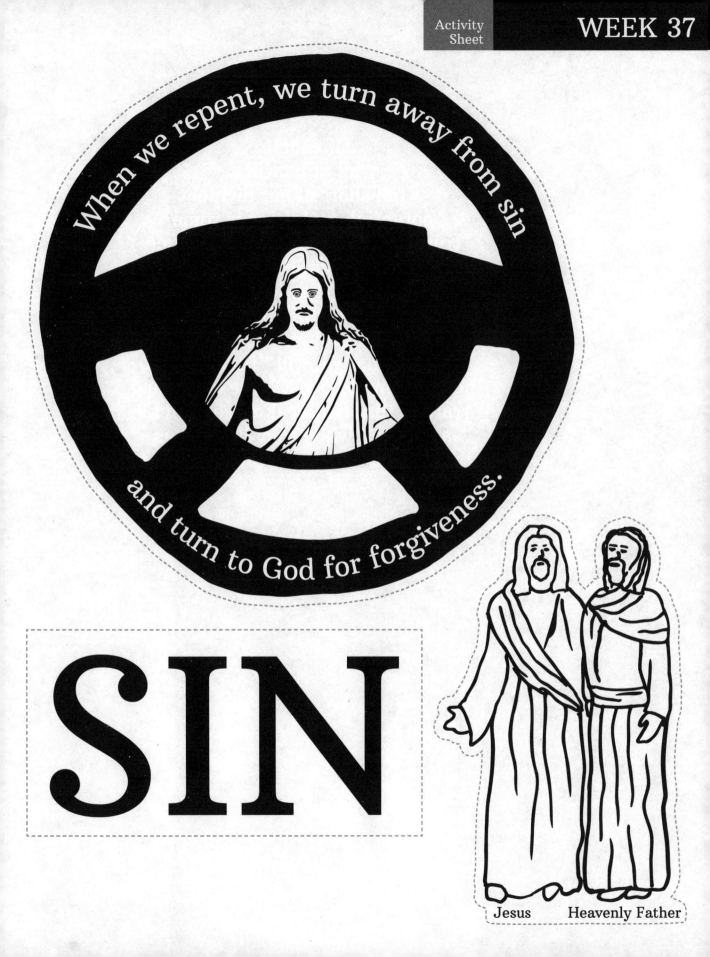

When we repent, we turn away from sin and turn to God for forgiveness.

SIN

Jesus   Heavenly Father

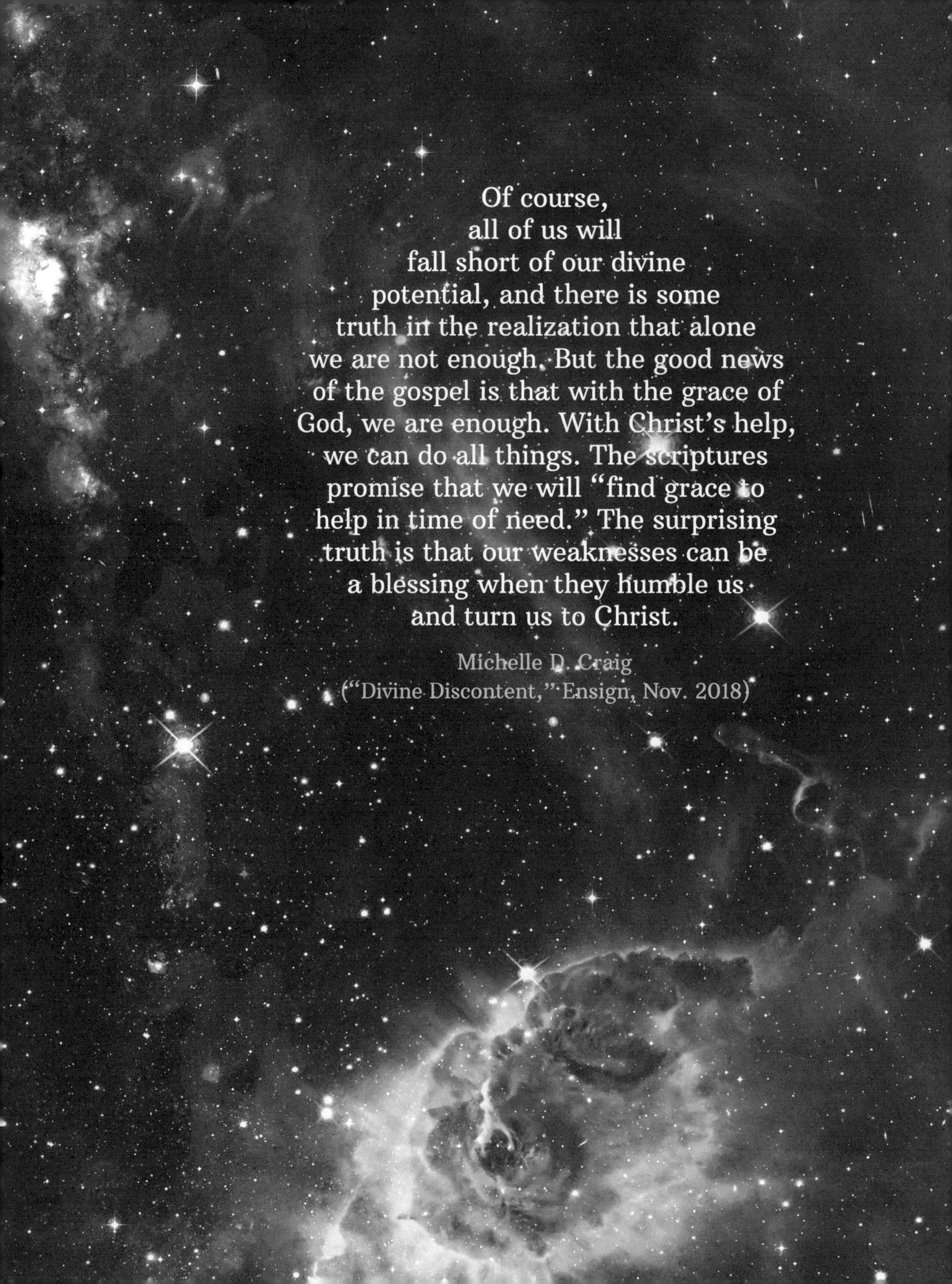

Of course,
all of us will
fall short of our divine
potential, and there is some
truth in the realization that alone
we are not enough. But the good news
of the gospel is that with the grace of
God, we are enough. With Christ's help,
we can do all things. The scriptures
promise that we will "find grace to
help in time of need." The surprising
truth is that our weaknesses can be
a blessing when they humble us
and turn us to Christ.

Michelle D. Craig
("Divine Discontent," Ensign, Nov. 2018)

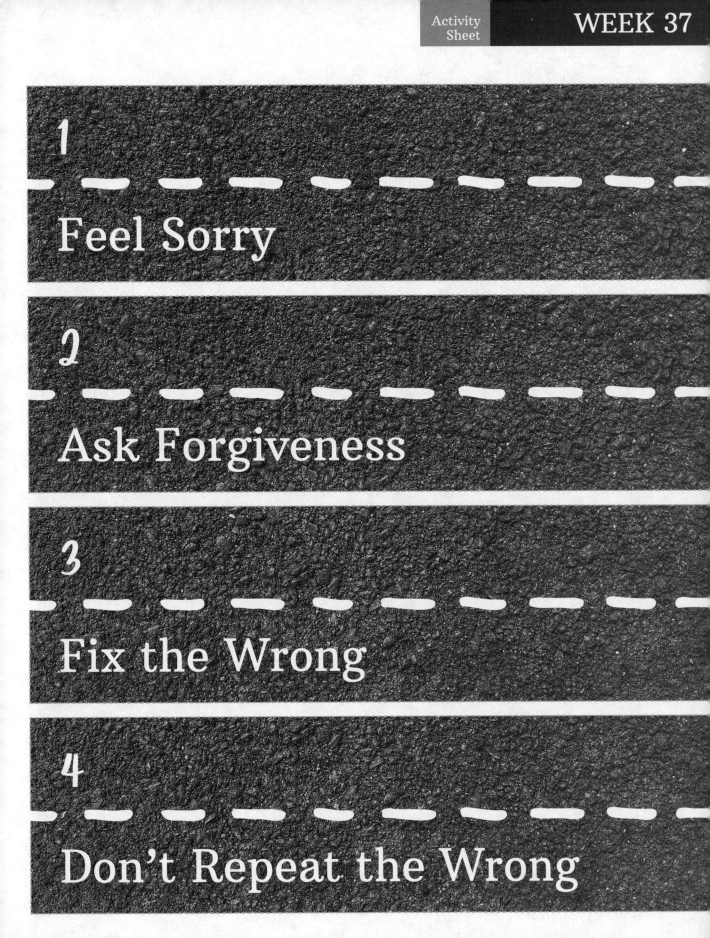

1

Feel Sorry

2

Ask Forgiveness

3

Fix the Wrong

4

Don't Repeat the Wrong

| GRUMPY | SILLY | PEACEFUL | CHEERFUL |
| SLEEPY | NERVOUS | CONFUSED | ANNOYED |

Hope you have a **happy** day!

Hope you have a **happy** day!

Hope you have a **happy** day!

Hope you have a **happy** day!

Hope you have a **happy** day!

Hope you have a **happy** day!

Hope you have a **happy** day!

Hope you have a **happy** day!

Cut
Fold

Tape or glue side flap closed

Fruits
OF THE
spirit

Galatians 5:22-23 | Contains 100% Goodness

Made with Real Fruit!

Tape or glue bottom flaps closed

Joy
Faith
Love
Longsuffering
Meekness
Peace
Temperance
Goodness
Gentleness

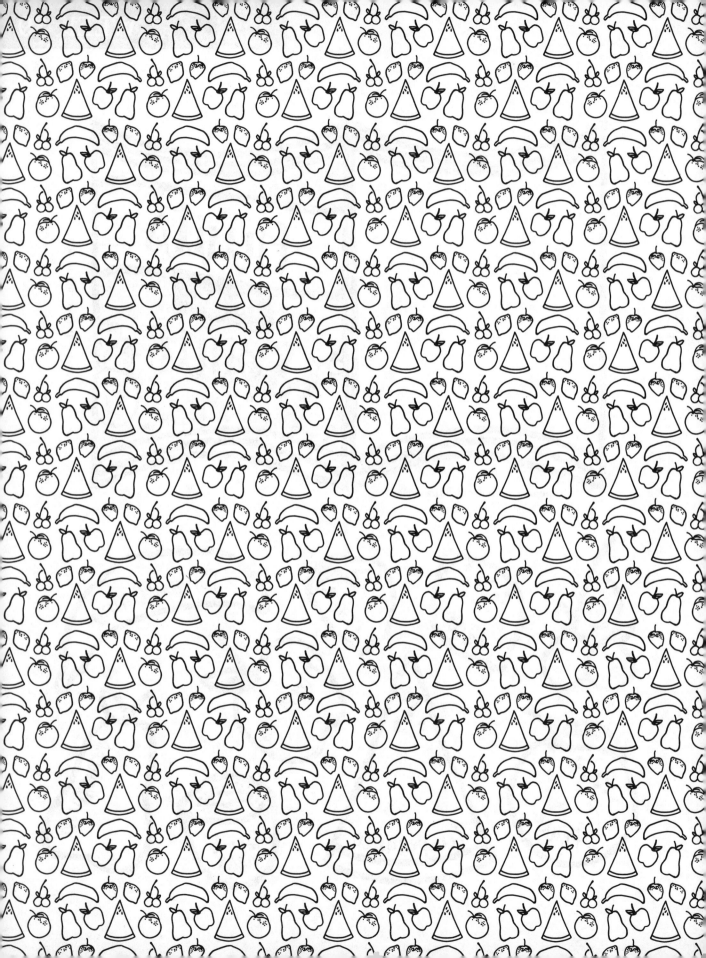

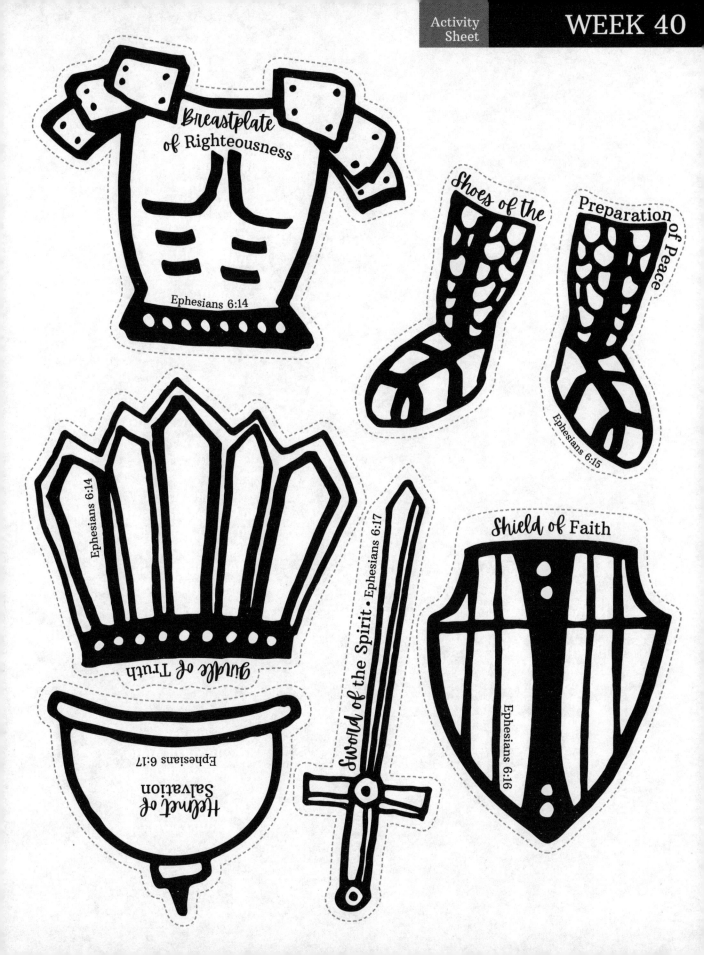

Breastplate of Righteousness
Ephesians 6:14

Shoes of the

Preparation of Peace
Ephesians 6:15

Ephesians 6:14

Guide of Truth

Ephesians 6:17

Helmet of Salvation

Sword of the Spirit • Ephesians 6:17

Shield of Faith
Ephesians 6:16

Name one
specific
way you
can follow
Jesus
Christ's
example
of
spreading
peace.

If a friend
was trying
to get you to
do something
you know you
shouldn't,
what would
you say to
them?

What truths have
you learned about
the Gospel of Jesus
Christ? How can these
truths help keep your
spirit safe?

Name two things
you can do to
keep your faith
growing strong.
How can your
faith protect you
from Satan?

Satan tries to trick us into thinking bad things are
good and good things are bad. How does the Spirit
help us know what is good and bad?

Salvation comes
to us through
Jesus Christ.
Name one reason
you're grateful
for Jesus.

Studying the word of Christ
Colossians 3:16

Doing good works
Colossians 1:10

Lying
Colossians 3:9

Humbleness
Colossians 3:12

Charity
Colossians 3:14

Longsuffering
Colossians 3:12

Forgiving
Colossians 3:13

Mean words
(Colossians 3:8)

Kindness
Colossians 3:12

Anger
Colossians 3:8

Meekness
Colossians 3:12

Mercy
Colossians 3:12

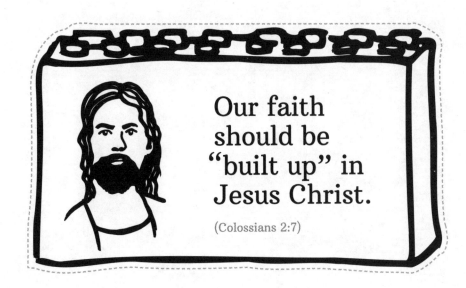

Our faith should be "built up" in Jesus Christ.

(Colossians 2:7)

1 Thessalonians 5:17 teaches us to "pray without ceasing." How can prayer help invite the feelings of the Spirit into our life? Light up one letter of the word "Spirit."

1 Thessalonians 5:14 tells us to "support the weak." Explain what this means and how doing so can help you feel the Spirit in your life. Light up one letter of the word "Spirit."

1 Thessalonians 5:14 tells us to "be patient toward all men." Share an example of a time when you were patient. Light up one letter of the word "Spirit."

1 Thessalonians 5:18 teaches, "In every thing give thanks." How can showing gratitude help us feel the Spirit in our lives? Tell each person in the room one reason why you're grateful for them. Light up one letter in the word "Spirit."

Uh-Oh!

You were mean to someone. Quench one Spirit letter.

Uh-Oh!

You decided to ignore your scriptures instead of reading them. Quench one Spirit letter.

Uh-Oh!

You told a lie. Quench one Spirit letter.

Uh-Oh!

You watched a video that chased away the Spirit. Quench one Spirit letter.

2 Thessalonians 3:13 teaches us to "be not weary in well doing." In your own words, explain what this means and how it helps invite the Spirit into your life. Light up one letter of the word "Spirit."

1 Thessalonians 5:20 teaches, "Despise not prophesyings." Name one teaching from a prophet or apostle that helps you feel the Spirit in your life. Light up one letter in the word "Spirit."

1 Thessalonians 5:21 tells us to "hold fast that which is good." Take one minute to list as many "good" things you can think of that are part of the gospel of Jesus Christ. How do these help you feel the Spirit in your life? Light up one letter in the word "Spirit."

Uh-Oh!

You skipped church because you wanted to play instead. Quench one Spirit letter.

Christ helps bring light into our lives through the Spirit.

Share one thing you'll do to invite Christ into your life. Then light up one of your Spirit letters!

Christ helps bring light into our lives through the Spirit.

Share one thing you'll do to invite Christ into your life. Then light up one of your Spirit letters!

Christ helps bring light into our lives through the Spirit.

Share one thing you'll do to invite Christ into your life. Then light up one of your Spirit letters!

1 Thessalonians 5:22 teaches, "Abstain from all appearance of evil." In your own words, explain what this means and how doing so can help us feel the Spirit. Light up one letter in the word "Spirit."

The
Scriptures
Make Me
Wise!

2 Timothy 3:15

The
Scriptures
Make Me
Wise!

2 Timothy 3:15

The
Scriptures
Make Me
Wise!

2 Timothy 3:15

The
Scriptures
Make Me
Wise!

2 Timothy 3:15

The
Scriptures
Make Me
Wise!

2 Timothy 3:15

The
Scriptures
Make Me
Wise!

2 Timothy 3:15

The
Scriptures
Make Me
Wise!

2 Timothy 3:15

The
Scriptures
Make Me
Wise!

2 Timothy 3:15

Scripture Reading Self-Report Card

Day
Sunday
Monday
Tuesday
Wednesday
Thursday
Friday
Saturday

Scripture Reading Self-Report Card

Day
Sunday
Monday
Tuesday
Wednesday
Thursday
Friday
Saturday

Scripture Reading Self-Report Card

Day
Sunday
Monday
Tuesday
Wednesday
Thursday
Friday
Saturday

Scripture Reading Self-Report Card

Day
Sunday
Monday
Tuesday
Wednesday
Thursday
Friday
Saturday

Scripture Reading Self-Report Card

Day
Sunday
Monday
Tuesday
Wednesday
Thursday
Friday
Saturday

Scripture Reading Self-Report Card

Day
Sunday
Monday
Tuesday
Wednesday
Thursday
Friday
Saturday

Scripture Reading Self-Report Card

Day
Sunday
Monday
Tuesday
Wednesday
Thursday
Friday
Saturday

Scripture Reading Self-Report Card

Day
Sunday
Monday
Tuesday
Wednesday
Thursday
Friday
Saturday

Hebrews 2:18

Christ Himself suffered being

_____ so that He is able

to _____ them that are tempted.

Hebrews 4:15

Christ is without _____.

Hebrews 4:16

Because of Christ, we can find grace to help us in time of _____.

Hebrews 5:8

Christ learned _____ by the things which He suffered.

Hebrews 5:9

Christ is an author of salvation unto all them that _____ _____.

Hebrews 1:2

God hath spoken unto us by His

_____.

Hebrews 1:3

Christ has the brightness of His (God's) glory, and the _____ _____ of His (God's) person.

Hebrews 2:9

Jesus was made a little lower than the

_____.

Hebrews 1:2

Christ is the heir of all things, by whom also He (God) made the _____.

Hebrews 1:6

All the angels of God _____ Him (Christ).

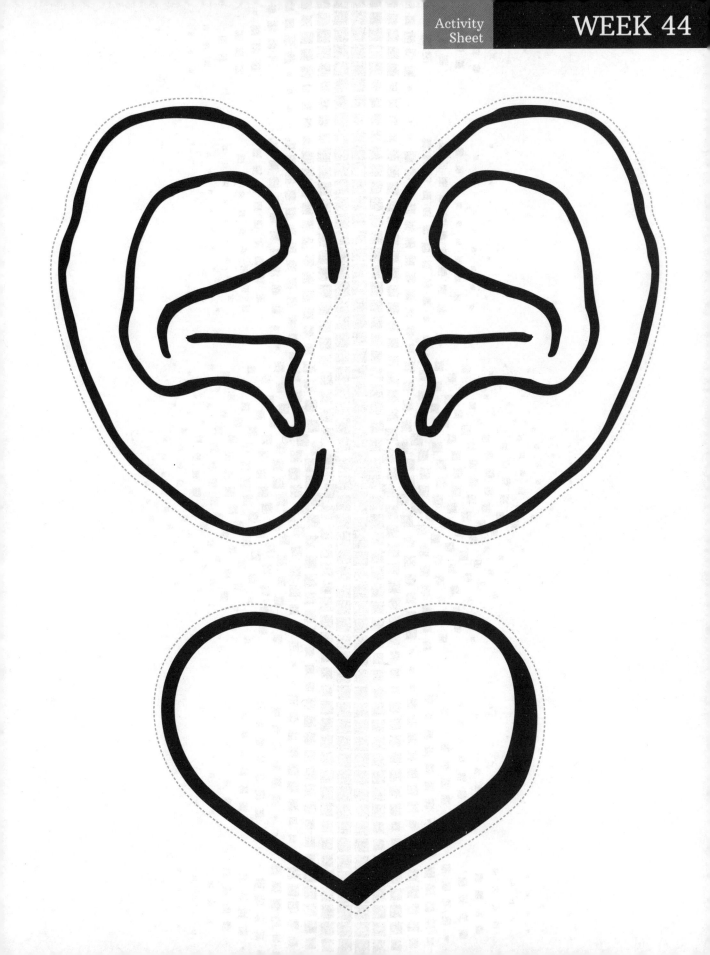

ENOCH

Hebrews 11:5–6

NOAH

Hebrews 11:7;
Genesis 6–8

ABRAHAM

Hebrews 11:8–10;
Hebrews 11:17–19;

SARAH

Hebrews 11:11;
Genesis 21:1–8

MOSES

Hebrews 11:23–29;
Exodus 14

RAHAB

Hebrews 11:31;
Joshua 2

DANIEL

Daniel 6:16–22

SHADRACH,
MESHACH, &
ABEDNEGO

Daniel 3:21–27

I will run with patience the race that is set before me.

121

Hebrews 12:1

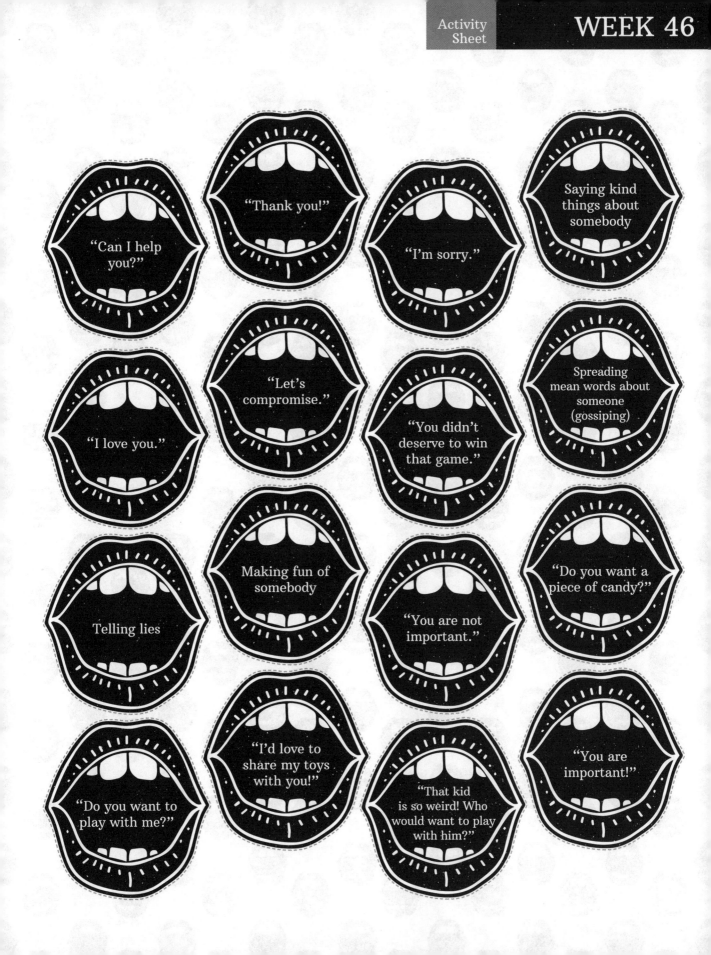

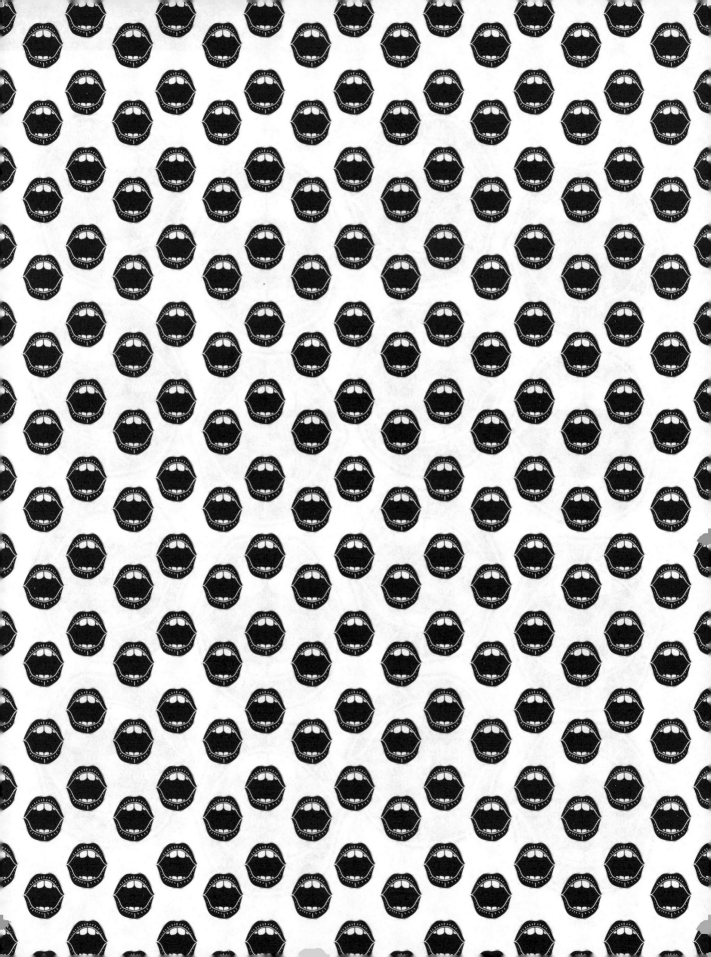

Fold so that the picture of Heavenly Father is on the inside of the shape. Do not tape or glue the edges. As each side flap is discussed and lifted, the picture of Heavenly Father will open up and become more clear.

Imagine you lived in Pergamos. People found out you believe in Christ. They told you that if you didn't stop worshiping Him, they would throw you into prison. What would you do?

A friend tells you you're wasting your time by going to church. What would you do?

A group of kids at school are laughing at stories from the scriptures and saying they couldn't be true. What would you do?

A teacher says that anyone who believes God is real must not be very smart. What would you do?

Someone tells you they can't be your friend because you believe differently than they do. What would you do?

Act out 2 different things you can do to strengthen your faith so that when pressure comes, you're still able to hold fast to your faith.

Some people are making fun of your church leaders. What would you do?

Someone dares you to rip up a picture of Jesus. What would you do?

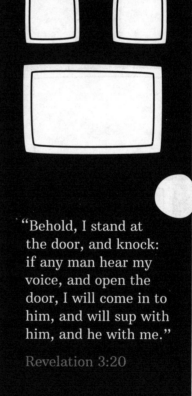

"Behold, I stand at the door, and knock: if any man hear my voice, and open the door, I will come in to him, and will sup with him, and he with me."

Revelation 3:20

Revelation 12:3, 9

3 And there appeared another wonder in heaven; and behold a great red dragon, having seven heads and ten horns, and seven crowns upon his heads.

9 And the great dragon was cast out, that old serpent, called the Devil, and Satan, which deceiveth the whole world: he was cast out into the earth, and his angels were cast out with him.

Revelation 5:6; Revelation 7:13–14

6 And I beheld, and, lo, in the midst of the throne and of the four beasts, and in the midst of the elders, stood a Lamb as it had been slain, having seven horns and seven eyes, which are the seven Spirits of God sent forth into all the earth.

13 And one of the elders answered, saying unto me, What are these which are arrayed in white robes? and whence came they?

14 And I said unto him, Sir, thou knowest. And he said to me, These are they which came out of great tribulation, and have washed their robes, and made them white in the blood of the Lamb.

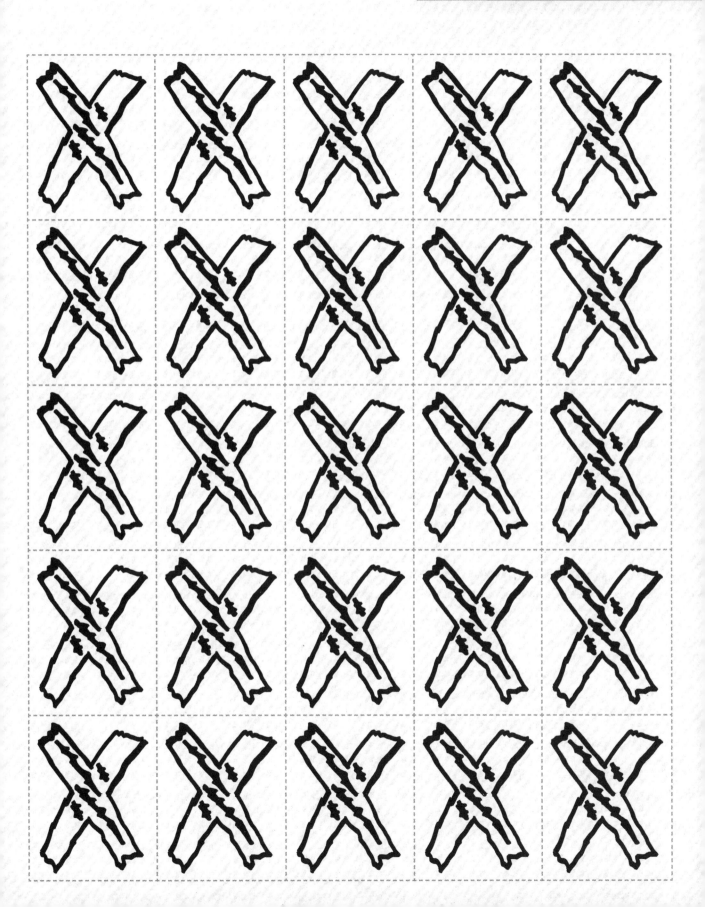

Luke 2:9-14

Luke 1:26-38
Luke 2:19

Matthew 1:18-25

Luke 2:7

Matthew 2:1-11

Luke 2:8, 15-17

Matthew 2:9-10

Inn
Luke 2:7

Luke 2:22-38

Revelation 17:5

"The Mother of Harlots and Abominations of the Earth"

Revelation 16:6

"They have shed the blood of saints and prophets"

Revelation 16:10

"Full of darkness; and they gnawed their tongues for pain"

Revelation 18:14

"All things which are dainty and goodly are departed from thee, and thou shalt find them no more at all"

Revelation 18:15

"Torment, weeping, and wailing"

Babylon

"The Holy City, New Jerusalem"

Revelation 21:2

Holy City Scripture Cards

"A pure river
of water of life,
clear as crystal,
proceeding out of
the throne of God
and of the Lamb."

Revelation 22:1

"The tree of life, which
bare twelve manner of
fruits, and yielded her
fruit every month: and
the leaves of the tree
were for the healing of
the nations."

Revelation 22:2

"And the city had
no need of the
sun, neither of the
moon, to shine in
it: for the glory of
God did lighten it,
and the Lamb is
the light thereof."

Revelation 21:23

"And I John saw
the holy city, new
Jerusalem, coming
down from God
out of heaven,
prepared as a bride
adorned for her
husband."

Revelation 21:2

"And God shall wipe
away all tears from their
eyes; and there shall be
no more death, neither
sorrow, nor crying,
neither shall there be any
more pain: for the former
things are passed away."

Revelation 21:4

"And the building
of the wall of it
was of jasper: and
the city was pure
gold, like unto
clear glass."

Revelation 21:18

"And the
foundations of the
wall of the city
were garnished
with all manner of
precious stones."

(Revelation 21:19)

"And the twelve gates
were twelve pearls; every
several gate was of one
pearl: and the street of
the city was pure gold, as
it were transparent glass."

(Revelation 21:21)

"God himself shall
be with them."

(Revelation 21:3)

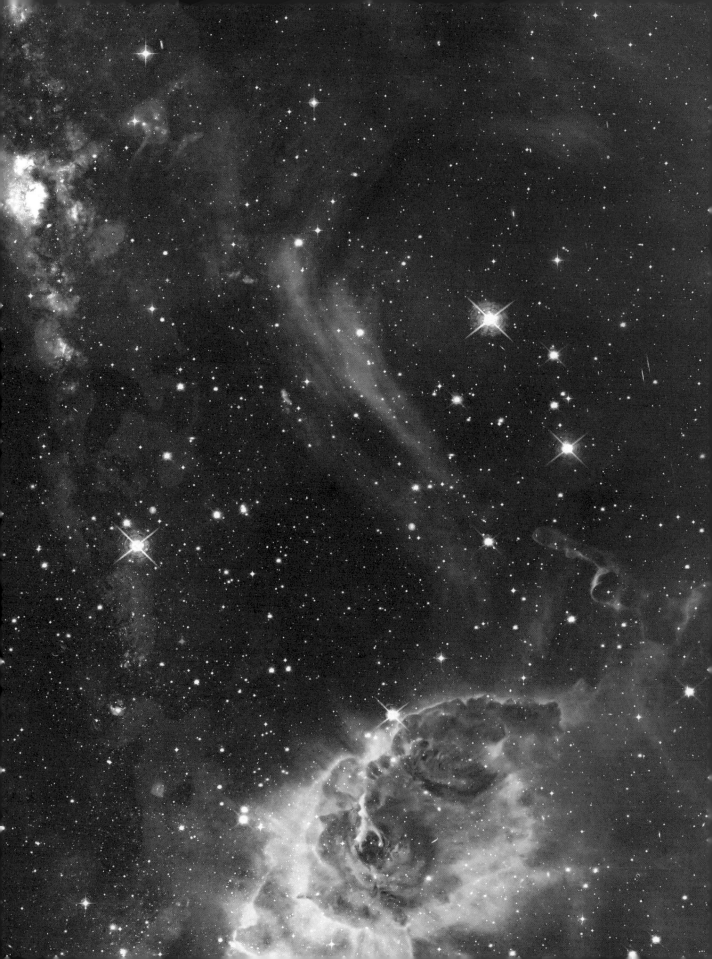

Hannah and Lucy are the whole reason this book was written. They frequently help think of fun ways to teach our lessons. Each of them wanted to share these additional activity ideas they came up with that could help us learn about Jesus Christ:

Hannah:

1 So mabe we could
2 read a card
3 about Jesus and we
4 could talk about
5 it. so im thinking
6 that we could like
7 get something that's
8 not ours and take
9 care of it. What if
10 we were playing
11 a game that you
12 like and take turns.

13 So mabe we
14 could do a
15 maze with Hevenly
16 father so like
17 we haft to find
18 him. So mobe we
19 could make a
20 candy path to
21 represent him. and
22 mabe we could draw
23 cards and read them.

Lucy:

"So someone sits in a chair. You have to have like 3 papers. And they have to close their eyes and they count to 1 and then when they open their eyes there's a picture of Jesus. Then after they see the picture of Jesus, they practice being reverent on the 3 pieces of paper. And they fold their arms and close their eyes."

"So someone has scriptures and we read some of the verses. And then we kind of like act the people out that we read about and then we're gonna read one of the verses about Esther and then King Solomon. Yep!"

"So this is kind of like a Monday activity. So we do have to go to the swimming pool and then we bring one of our dolls and make it get baptized. K! And then after the doll gets baptized, we have a big celebration because the doll got baptized."

"So . . . have a hair clip. And then we pretend it's pinching someone, and then one of us come and help the person who got pinched by it. Like if they got sunburned or if someone was saying something mean or if they falled, we could help them."

"So someone's jumping on the bed. Not Hannah's bed because we would bonk our head on the roof! So I have to jump on Mom's bed, and then one of us roll off the bed. And so first Daddy rolls off, and then Mom, and then Hannah, and then me (Lucy). And then when we all roll off of the bed, then we go into the living room and jump off of the couch. And then we say, 'No way! No way! No way! No way!' A million times. We shouldn't jump on the couches or the bed. Because Jesus teaches us to try not to get hurt."

52
WEEKS
of NEW
TESTAMENT
ACTIVITIES